I0390536

Gen X & Millennials: Protect your Money and Prosper

Gen X & Millennials: Protect your Money and Prosper

Financial Advice the media won't tell you.

Chad A Walker

The information provided within this book is strictly for educational purposes. If you wish to apply ideas contained in this book, you are taking full responsibility for your actions. The author has made every effort to ensure the accuracy of the information within this book was correct at time of publication. The author does not assume and hereby disclaims any liability to any party for any loss, damage, or disruption caused by errors or omissions, whether such errors or omissions from accident, negligence, or any other cause.

There are no representations or warranties, express or implied, about the completeness, accuracy, reliability, suitability or availability with respect to the information, products, services, or related graphics contained in this book for any purpose.

The author is not providing individual financial, investment, or tax advice. Any use of this information is at your own risk.

Copyright © 2017 by Chad A Walker

All rights reserved. This book or any portion thereof may not be reproduced or used in any manner whatsoever without the express written permission of the publisher except for the use of brief quotations in a book review.

Authored by: Chad A. Walker, CPA, MBA

Edited by: Sandy Fox, www.investmentcopy.com

Cover by: Jason Smart, Smarty Design Co

ISBN: 1541060598
ISBN 13: 9781541060593
Published by: Coast 2 Coast Financial
www.coast2coastfinancial.com

Thank you to Porter Stansberry, Stansberry Research; Mark Ford, Palm Beach Research Group; Bill Bonner, Bonner and Partners; and Craig Ballantyne, Early to Rise.

I've yet to personally meet any of you. But through reading your work and teachings, you've opened my eyes on how to get ahead in this uncertain world. And allowed clarity in my life so that I can help others learn how to protect and prosper financially themselves.

Thank you to my friends, family, and colleagues that have listened to me over the years as I developed and refined these ideas. Your open ears and minds have helped guide me towards the vision of how to clearly explain this complex and contradicting information, so that those not involved or interested in finances can understand and implement.

Table of Contents

To anyone who is working hard and earning a good income but **doesn't feel like they're getting anywhere financially or closer to their retirement goals.**

To anyone who doesn't enjoy finance but know they need to prepare themselves financially.

To anyone who has a hard time trusting mainstream financial outlets because it feels like they're just out to profit off of you.

To anyone who knows the world has changed, that you can't follow your parent's model to retirement, and that you need to begin thinking differently.

❀ ❀ ❀

Chapter 1

Intro to Financial Advice, Asset Allocation and Long Term Wealth Building

Finding simple advice you can trust

This book will explain why you must take control of your financial future. You'll learn how easy it is to take immediate action to protect and profit in the coming years. It's for people ages 25-45 who don't have lots of money invested but do have more earning years. By the end, you'll know what's occurring in the connected world economy and, unlike most people; you'll recognize the trends and be ready to profit from them.

Before I get into specifics, let's review the keys to understanding and trusting the financial advice you're receiving.

In my Free Report, *Five Keys: Can You Trust Your Financial Advice?*, I explain five keys for knowing if the financial advice you receive is operating in your best interest. You can find the report on my website, www.coast2coast-financial.com, but we'll review the basics here as well.

The key is determining how the person giving you financial advice is getting paid.

Certified financial planners collect fees on a flat fee basis. Their profit source? Getting more clients. They are so connected into mainstream finance that they'll miss the protection and profitable strategies that can maximize your long term wealth.

Most of their referrals come from accounting and tax friends, investment managers they work closely with, and lawyer friends. So client referrals are less essential to them.

Investment managers get commissions for assets under management. Their number one goal is to maximize the amount of assets under their management. This increases fees. On paper it appears the better they do for you the more people who will want them to manage their assets. But their large fees eat at returns and ultimately they earn a management fee, even if your portfolio loses money.

CNBC. Fox Business News. All mainstream news outlets. Do you pay directly for these channels? Nope, they're free (included in your TV subscription). And they say all day long how they're working hard to help you make money. How are they paid? By the advertisers. What are the typical commercials? TD Ameritrade. Charles Schwab. Interactive Brokers. ETF funds. I could go on and on.

These programs are motivated to get you trading so their advertisers can earn money. And since this information is free, everyone has access to it. Can you make money and get ahead while doing what everyone else is doing? No. That's why there's the 1% and there's the 99%. The 99% do what everyone else is doing and never gets ahead. The 1% do something else.

Hedge funds, portfolio managers, and anyone else who runs a fund you invest your hard-earned money with. Similar to general investment managers, they want assets in their fund. Even worse, they're sometimes compensated for tracking an index or trying to beat an index. Beating an index that goes negative even if their own fund earns a negative return is still a win.

Do you want someone managing your money who thinks a negative return is good? And that negative return earns them a bonus? I don't.

Online brokerage accounts and full-service brokers are necessary for trading and I use many of them for my personal investments. But I don't take advice from any of them or use any of their research tools. All their tools are structured to get you trading. TD Ameritrade charges $9.99 per trade. They make no money off me having hundreds of thousands of dollars in their account unless I trade.

They call me several times a year trying to get me to use their trading platforms so I execute more trades. This isn't in my best interest. It's in their best interest.

See the free report for full details and the five keys but you get the point. You need to understand the financial interest of the person giving you advice.

What's My Profit?

So before I go any further, what is my financial interest in giving you this advice and writing this book? You deserve to know. You can read my full story and bio on my website, but I'll answer briefly here.

First, I have a great paying job that I enjoy and it earns me enough money to live the life I choose. I want to sell this book for three reasons. One, the price of the book will allow me to cover my expenses in creating, editing, designing, and maintaining the book, reports, website, and weekly newsletter. This is vital, as it lets you remain up to date on what's happening around the connected financial world.

Two, if I didn't charge for the book it would be dismissed as not being valuable. People would download it and not read it. You just spent your hard earned money for this book, I hope that motivates you to read the book and implement the ideas.

They are that important.

Three, earning a little revenue from the book allows me to continue to re-invest in more newsletters and more investment education. So I can continue to perform my role of converting complex, somewhat contradictory information into easy, simple, concise advice for you. You'll get this information through my weekly **free** newsletter, subsequent books and reports.

At the end of the book I give reviews and recommendations where you can find specific stock picks, investing education, and wealth building tools. Every service written about in that section, I subscribe to fully and read regularly.

I commit to you that my reviews are honest. Sometimes I tell you the flaws in the newsletter and why not to subscribe. I don't want you to subscribe to every newsletter like I do. I want you to subscribe to the specific newsletter that fits your profile and will help you succeed.

I subscribe to and read them all so I can explain them to you simply. You should only subscribe if you want to learn more details and specific recommendations.

Finally, I'm doing this because I've already done well in my life. I've made money through my career as a Certified Public Accountant (CPA). And then I've taken that money and used my abilities to study financial and economic trends to structure a portfolio that will allow me to be financially free for the rest of my life. I feel lucky to have natural abilities to understand the com-plexities of investing.

I want you to have that same opportunity, but I understand not everyone has the same skills as me. I certainly don't have the same skills as you. So I want to provide you the opportunity to implement safe, protective yet prosperous financial strategies so you have plenty of time to focus on what you're good at and enjoy.

Every one of us is an individual and has different interests and skills. One of my skills happens to align with my interests. I enjoy doing this and want you to enjoy doing what you do. And if we all are able to do what we enjoy doing, this world will be a better place.

This is my selfish motivation. I want to live in a world with more happy people doing what they enjoy. Not burdened by financial struggles. If I can help more people achieve this outcome, it will make my life better and more enjoyable.

In summary, go back and read my free report on how to know if you can trust the financial advice you're receiving. Go to my website and read my biography and story so you better understand my motivation. I want to help those that want to improve their life.

Let Your Asset Allocation Build for Maximum Long Term Wealth

Before you begin implementing any investment strategy or long term wealth building tools, you must understand asset allocation. Asset allocation allows you to have a portfolio that can handle all types of markets; side markets, up markets, and down markets.

In simple terms, asset allocation spreads your investments across different asset classes that don't move in the same direction all the time. Mainstream finance will tell you a selection of stocks, bonds, and cash is a good allocation. If you work with an advisor from an insurance company, they'll tell you insurance should be part of your allocation but remember their financial motivation.

Cash is protection and stocks typically go up when bonds may go down. And bonds go up when stocks go down, because of their fixed interest rate payments.

The idea is that if one portion of your portfolio goes down, you only lose some money. The other portion of your portfolio may not drop or even go up which offsets the downside of the other portion.

In order to help you understand asset allocation, I wrote a report detailing my proprietary asset allocation strategy. It's designed for individuals with over 20 years until retirement and willing to take a long term approach to wealth-building. I call this strategy, *Let Your Asset Allocation Build*. The report can be purchased from my website, www.coast2coastfinancial.com. If you're early in your wealth building, this strategy will accelerate your progress and is easy to implement.

Let me give you a quick overview of the report.

Almost everyone involved in the financial, investing, and economic industries agrees that asset allocation is important. It's considered the #1 way to ensure long term investing success. Most financial outlets have slightly different allocations but in general they're all pretty similar.

Tony Robbins goes through various asset classes and provides a general strategy in his popular book, *Money: Master the Game*. In general most mainstream outlets suggest allocating between stocks, bonds, cash, real estate, and precious metals. The specific allocations differ based upon age, as your risk profile changes as you age.

I don't disagree with any of these. However, they're all flawed for one simple reason and this is the secret to my *Let Your Asset Allocation Build* strategy.

They're all based upon you already having wealth. If you have $5M or are 65 years old and have enough retirement funds, great. Find one of these strategies you trust, implement it and you'll be fine.

But let's be honest. Most of you reading this book (myself included) are between 25-45 years old and are in our peak earning years. We have saved some money in our retirement funds, but have not yet saved even $1M, yet alone $5M. And we have over 20 years until retirement.

These typical asset allocation strategies do a disservice to you. If you were to implement any one of those strategies immediately, you'd be taking your hard-earned but limited savings and forcing yourself to buy certain invest-ments. **Regardless of whether they are cheap!**

That's in bold because it's the secret to my strategy. You don't need to be perfectly allocated right now if you're not yet wealthy, just getting started building your wealth, and in your peak earning years.

Otherwise you're setting yourself up for disappointing returns by buying certain asset classes that are overvalued. You can afford to go overweight in certain asset classes if they're cheap today.

Then as they rise in value and other asset classes become cheap, you sell the profits you made from going overweight in your portfolio in cheap assets initially, and use the proceeds to buy the other asset classes that are now cheap.

As we'll discuss in the next section, all asset classes are cyclical and go through cheap periods and expensive periods. Your hard-earned, limited cap-ital should only buy what's cheap. This will allow you to exceed the returns of mainstream financial advisors, who may or may not have good intentions, telling you to allocate your assets immediately.

To succeed, you have to make sure you understand the risks, have an end goal in place so you can make the correct decisions, and do a little research (like reading this book). This will allow you to be confident what you're buying is truly cheap.

You'll find more details in my proprietary asset allocation report, *Let Your Asset Allocation Build.* This special report is an important tool you should read several times and make sure you understand. Here you'll find specifics on how to create your own plan by figuring out your goals and assessing your risks.

We're almost ready to wrap up this chapter and move onto understanding stock market booms, crashes, and the most recent financial crisis of 2008. Before we do, let's talk about wealth building.

Two Keys to Building Long Term Wealth

Understanding how to get trusted financial advice and asset allocation are the building blocks to wealth building. However, those things alone will not get you long term wealth.

You need to do two very important items for yourself immediately. They're not hard; they just take discipline and an open mind.

First, you must have capital to invest. Even if you have trustworthy financial advice and my proprietary asset allocation strategy to maximize returns, they don't do any good without capital. You have to make the commitment and implement the discipline to earn and save money.

There are two simple ways to increase investable funds. Earn more money. Spend less money. It's easy but most people don't want to do it. You need to understand that a little sacrifice today, such as working one more hour a week (or one more hour a day), can make you more valuable in your job to get higher raises or if you're hourly earn a little extra income. Save 100% of this extra money.

A little sacrifice in cutting back on expenses and saving 100% of it today is easy. This may sound hard to you because you love that extra free time and you love that Starbucks Mocha Frappuccino. But a regular coffee with cream and sugar and one less hour of TV time from spending less and working longer, can provide you a little more investable capital.

Multiply those hours and savings by 20 years. Add in trusted financial advice and my allocation building strategy and those little amounts of money may well create the freedom you desire. And you'll get even more benefits than you can imagine right now— vacation homes, early retirement, kid's college. **You just have to trust that every step you're taking today, impacts the life you'll have tomorrow.**

I know it's difficult to think 20 years from now, but there are over 7,000 days between today and 20 years from now. If you make little sacrifices today and implement the additional capital wisely over 7,000 **compounded** days, your life will be exponentially better. I promise.

I'll lay out 10 steps you can implement immediately to begin saving more in Appendix 2.

In Appendix 3, I'll recommend some wonderful newsletters that offer great wealth building tips for saving money, changing how you think about saving money, and even ways to create additional income streams. I've implemented several of these personally. Yes, I gave up some things a few years ago, and even today, that were difficult initially. But I'm already reaping the rewards of the sacrifices and it's motivating me to sacrifice even more today for 20 years from now. Plus after a little time, it doesn't even feel like a sacrifice. It just becomes a great life!

Second, you have to begin thinking differently than everyone else. If you're not in the 1%, you're in the 99%. If you're in the 1%, you don't need to read this book.

So that means we're all in the 99%. And if you're in the 99%, everyone you talk to, communicate with, and all the news/information you watch/read/take-in is the same as everyone else in the 99%.

If you only listen to what everyone else is doing, how will you ever get out of the 99%? You won't. Yes, you could be an exception who wins the lottery or invents the next Facebook. But I know that's not going to be me. And probably not you either.

This doesn't mean you won't have a good or nice life. But it does mean you won't ever really get ahead. Or get as far ahead as you could.

To get ahead and break out of the crowd, you have to open your mind to new ideas. Be okay thinking differently than anyone else you come in contact with or what the news tells you.

Trust me. This is sometimes lonely and very difficult. I went through some health issues because I had no one to talk to when I began doing this. But now just a few short years later, everyone who didn't accept what I was doing is now interested in it. I'm writing this book to help you avoid some of my struggles.

You have someone to talk to. You have my weekly newsletter to read for free. You can submit questions to me. You're not going at it alone. You just have to be prepared to hear all mainstream media contradicting what you're doing. And you have to expect friends and family will not understand what you're doing.

Soon enough, they'll see you breaking from the crowd and begin asking questions. You'll go from being on the outside to being the person everyone wants to talk to about financial success. But you have to be prepared. It's difficult to change your way of thinking to break away from what everyone else is doing.

This book, my free newsletter, and all my special reports will help. But they will do nothing if you don't commit to having an open mind and the self-discipline to stick to the convictions that you'll learn.

By reading my reports, newsletter and this book, I promise you'll know more than 99% of everyone you talk to, what you hear on the news about how the connected world economies work, and how to profit from understanding market cycles.

If you understand how to find and receive trusted financial advice, my proprietary asset allocation strategy, and the two secrets to long term wealth building you're at a special place, my friend. You've already come further along than anyone else you know. And we're only though the first chapter!

Now we'll move on to explain simply and concisely what's happening around the world economy, how to protect yourself, and ultimately how to prosper.

Chapter 2

● ● ●

Stock Market Booms and Busts

Protect yourself and profit from these inevitable, easy to understand cycles

Over the long term the stock market typically goes up. If you look at the chart of the S&P 500 shown below, it looks like it just keeps going up. The average annual return from 1928-2015 is between 9-11%, depending upon how you measure it.

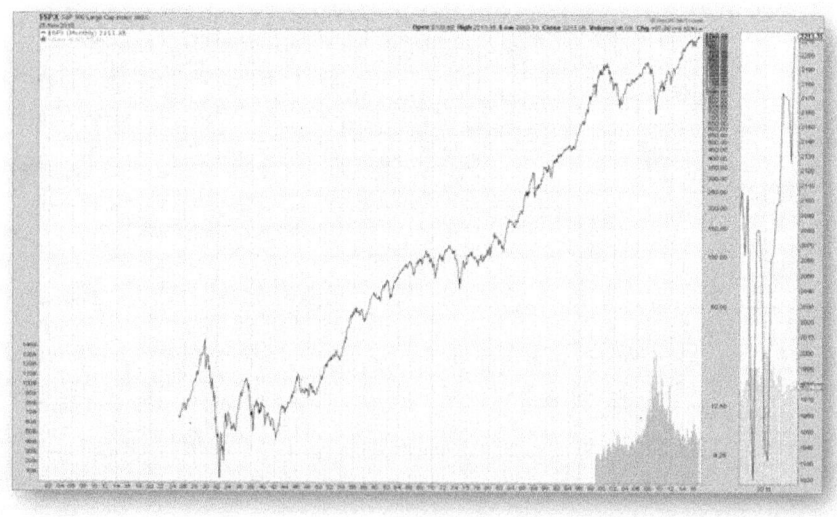

Not bad. You'll hear a lot of financial advisors say this is why you need to invest in stocks for the long term. Buy some of the index funds they manage and sit and wait.

They'll tell you this means if you're 35 years old and invest your 401k of $200k in a S&P 500 Index fund, that were to return on average 10% a year, you'd have $3.1M when you're 65 and you'll have $8.2M when you're 75. That's pretty darn good and very appealing.

But just because the S&P 500 returns on average 10%, it doesn't mean you'll earn 10% per year. If you look closer at the chart above, specifically in 2001 and 2008, you'll notice large drops in the S&P 500. By just buying and holding, your returns are diminished. Your portfolio will not actually return what was calculated above with the **average** return.

For example assume year 1 the S&P 500 index fund goes up 10%, year 2 down 10%, and year 3 up 30%. Your average return would be 10% per year. Assuming your $200k earned 10% per year in this index fund as your advisor will suggest, would amount to $266,200 after 3 years. But **average** does not take the change in compounding on rising and falling amounts into account. In reality the $200k earning 10% in year 1, losing 10% in year 2, and earning 30% in year 3 only gets you $257,400. It's still an increase but not as large as you'll be led to believe.

It also doesn't account for **when** you start investing. And it doesn't account for recent lower returns. The most recent 15 year average was only 5%. The most recent 10 year average was 8.5%. With low interest and inflation, the next 20-30 years may only return 5%.

Say you actually invested $200k in the S&P 500 in 2005 and got the actual return of each year for the next 10 years. And then for the next 20-30 years your return on average was 5% or 8.5%.

In 30 years your $200k is worth only $1.2M at 5% and $2.2M at 8.5%. In 40 years your $200k is worth $2.2M at 5% and $5M at 8.5%. That's still not bad. But notice, it's much lower than if you earned the 100 year average return of the stock market every year. In reality, you don't earn an average return. You earn the actual return, which has increases and decreases every year.

Stay with me. I want to explain this in a bit more detail, so you'll see why there's a better way.

Suppose we took the last 15 years of **actual** returns and projected them forward for the next 30 or 40 years. This way your portfolio will get ups and downs as opposed to a nice "average" return which skews calculations. Now your $200k will only be worth $850k after 30 years and $976k after 40 years.

That's not too exciting is it? Per my asset allocation guide, does that meet your retirement goal and let you live the lifestyle you want?

Admittedly, that's assuming you put no more money in after 35. Hopefully you're planning to invest more.

But let's leave out adding additional money for simplicity. Does that end amount meet your needed funds you calculated in the asset allocation guide to retire on your expected standard of living?

It may, I don't know. Only you can know if that's acceptable. And of course that's assuming you're disciplined to keep your money invested over that long period of time and don't sell if there is a market crash.

Why am I telling you this? Because I want you to understand your odds of actually getting the "average return" of the historical S&P 500 is not realistic. And while the long term view of the stock market is typically that it goes up, buying and holding for the long term doesn't produce the great returns you may expect.

This is because while it typically goes up over the long term, corrections or large declines can set you back drastically. And due to the human emotion of fear, many individual investors decide to sell immediately after a correction and miss out on the start of the next rise. This causes you to earn **even less** than the last example I shared. You could end up with negative returns.

What if you only bought stocks when they were low? And you sold stocks when they were high? Now I'm not suggesting you can predict when it's at the highs or at the lows. But you can understand when it's cheap or nearing lows and when it's expensive and nearing highs.

Back in 2001 and 2008, it was obvious stocks were expensive. But due to the human emotion of greed, the fact stocks had been rising for years, and mainstream media saying you need to be in the market, most people didn't trim their position or sell out of the market.

Then in 2009, it was obvious stocks were cheap. But due to the human emotion of fear, the fact people just lost a huge percentage of their portfolio, and mainstream media saying you should not be in the market, most people didn't buy stocks.

Please don't sell everything when you believe the market is expensive.

I'm explaining this rather as a point that stocks get expensive and stocks get cheap— even though over long term history stocks tend to go up. And if you're disciplined and buy only when they're cheap and sell when they're expensive, you'll maximize returns.

However, if you bought a great dividend paying company that you truly expect to be around forever, you wouldn't want to sell them even when the share price got really high. This would interrupt the compounding ability of the dividend.

For instance, Warren Buffet bought Coca-Cola between 1987-1989. He has not sold any shares and says he never will. Stansberry Research reports "Adjusted for splits and dividends already paid, Buffet paid $2.50 per share for his stock in 1988….In 2015, Coke paid out $1.32 in dividends per share."[1]

Think about this. Each year Buffet is basically getting paid through a dividend 50% of what he paid for his Coke stock. And that doesn't factor in the capital gains he'd receive if he sold Coke at the $41 it trades at today. Why would he sell it when every two years he earns his initial investment back? And since Coke has paid a dividend every year since 1970, Buffet has confidence they'll continue to pay a dividend.

So that is even better than buying and selling. And now consider the fact that the dividend percentage has increased. You may have heard of the power of compounding interest before. Well reinvesting dividends works the same way.

But don't run out and by Coke today. You have to buy Coke when it's the right price. Remember from the asset allocation strategy, we want to buy the assets for our long term allocation when they are cheap to maximize returns.

Coke is not cheap today. So we need to be patient and wait for it to become cheap, then buy.

This also doesn't mean you should sell Coke today. If you bought Coke cheap in the past and are reinvesting dividends, by all means hold it for the long term. Don't interrupt the compounding. My focus in this book is to get you to understand how to think about long term investing and only buying assets when they are cheap.

---

1 Porter Stansberry. Special Report. March 3, 2016. "How to Find the Best Government-Proof, Inflation-Proof, Crisis-Proof, Bear-Market Proof 'Magic' Stocks Right now."

What I just shared is not intended to give you a specific strategy but to reinforce what you should have learned in the asset allocation guide. Only buy the assets for your long term portfolio when those assets are cheap.

And I'm also trying to help you understand that assets go up (get expensive) and they go down (get cheap).

So don't feel like you have to buy when you see things going up. They'll come back down. This is the first part of the contrarian view and open mind you'll need to have. When the market is going up, everyone gets excited. Mainstream media, your broker, and everyone you know think you have to be buying.

That's the mentality you have to learn to step away from. If everyone thinks you need to be buying, how are you going to get ahead? If everyone is buying, where is the opportunity? You need to understand if everyone is buying, who is left to buy more to keep the price rising?

But once everyone stops buying, there are a lot of people who can sell to drive the price down.

The key here is to understand you don't need to do what everyone else is doing. You can develop strategies to build your long term asset allocation and buy into those strategies only when they are cheap.

This book is not going to discuss all strategies available and how you can implement them. It's best to start with the most effective and most profitable one. Most strategies cost a lot to use, but this one you can begin using with a small amount of money.

As we move forward I'll discuss the best strategy right now that is so cheap, it can create huge returns. And even if I'm wrong, it's so cheap you are very unlikely to lose money.

Before I proceed, let's recap and define contrarian.

Contrarian basically means you do the opposite of others. This is how we get ahead. If everyone is buying something, you don't. And when everyone else is scared to buy something, you look into it.

Remember what I said in Chapter 1. It's tough to develop this mentality but it is key to maximizing your long term wealth building to break out and get ahead.

If you're willing to do what everyone else is **not** doing, that gives you opportunity. Remember, there is only 1% at the top for a reason. So if you begin to do things different from the 99%, you give yourself a shot of big returns and moving towards the top 1%.

If you do what everyone else is doing, you'll stay in the 99%.

The idea of this book is to change your mentality about long term wealth building by explaining in simple terms how things really work. Then I'll finish by explaining the best strategy today for a really cheap asset.

My newsletter and future books will continue to update you on other strategies, like buying Coke when it's cheap and reinvesting the dividends. Look for my newsletter and I promise I'll explain these kinds of strategies when you can use them… like when Coke is cheap.

Why Market Swings?

Why do stocks, commodities, and even houses go up and down, in these big cycles? The answer revolves a lot around groupthink and the misleading information mainstream financial media gives you.

When everything is going up, groups of people get excited, begin investing, making money, and become blinded to the fact that things could ever change. Then on top of that, the media and mainstream financial outlets start talking about how you need to get in on the trend. How everyone is making money and if you're not in, you're missing out.

Just remember, they make money in ways that don't align with your financial interests. If things are just going up, it's easier to promote them and to make money off of you— even if you shouldn't be buying.

Your friends and family start saying how much money they've made in something and tell you that you need to get in. Everyone becomes blind to the risks and keeps buying, buying, buying. This is driven by one of the top two emotions in humans, greed.

But remember, when there is nobody left to buy, can it go higher? This fuels extremes on the high-end.

Then there is the low-end. When the market is overblown, something triggers a shift. When the trigger happens, buying slows. Then selling starts.

When people start selling, the prices get driven down. This creates losses in portfolios. People hate losses in their portfolios and fear sets in. They begin to sell because they are afraid of experiencing bigger losses. This leads to more and more selling and a steep drop in prices.

Since selling is now the popular theme, mainstream media and financial outlets begin talking about how nobody should hold things and everyone needs to sell. Your broker begins telling you to sell because they don't want to be the one responsible for you holding something that goes down more. Notice that their motives are about themselves, not about whether it's in your best interest to sell.

Next thing you know, prices are really low and extremely undervalued. This is driven by the other top emotion in humans, fear. Fear of losing **more** money.

Now, nobody is buying and everyone wants to sell. But once everyone has sold, who is left to sell and drive prices lower? This is why we reach bottoms and prices then return upward.

You don't have to live in this bubble/bust cycle. You can be more informed. This also means that anytime you buy an asset, know your exit strategy.

For instance, if you buy Coke when it gets cheap with the intention of compounding dividends for 30 years, you will not sell when it gets high and you will not sell when it drops. You'll be confident knowing your strategy of compounding dividends will work over the long term. Just like Buffet and why he says he'll never sell a share.

You will not be swayed by the misleading information in the mainstream outlets.

This boom/bust cycle we discussed actually creates the opportunities you need to buy things cheaply to achieve your long term asset allocation goals.

Let's take a look at a real world scenario that happened back in 2008 so you can see how you can use it to your advantage.

FINANCIAL CRISIS OF 2008: How it could have been predicted and how you can learn from it to profit in the next crisis

How can 2008 help you understand how it was possible to see a price drop coming? How could you have known to get out of investments (i.e. take gains on things you bought cheaply)? And once the crash occurred, how could you have known to buy extremely cheap assets for your long term portfolio?

Please don't read this and get frustrated that you didn't see the crash coming. Don't feel like you missed out on the incredible opportunities created by the crash to buy into your long term asset allocation really cheap. I was impacted and didn't take advantage just like you. But I used it to learn how to protect and profit for the next time.

The specific assets that became cheap may not ever get as cheap as they were but they'll get cheap again. This always happens because the 99% are always driven by greed and fear. It's natural. So opportunities will always be created.

I don't want you to feel like you missed something. I'm trying to teach you so you can begin implementing going forward. The opportunity that exists today may be better than anything you missed out on back in 2008. So learn from this story so you can take advantage of the opportunity that exists today.

When you think of the financial crisis of 2007-2009, you probably recall the housing crash and stock market crash.

You may have even lost a lot of money in your portfolio or had a home that became "worth" less than you paid. If you didn't, you probably know someone who did.

That is the take away I hear most people talk about. How housing crashed and the stock market crashed.

If you're like me, you were still in the early stages of your career and didn't have much money to lose. And... you probably didn't take advantage of the opportunities to make money and buy cheap assets after the crash because you were not prepared. But this crash moved me to research, study, and become more prepared to handle the ups and downs of markets.

In 2007-2009 I bought into the media-promoted dream of house ownership. At that time everyone thought the key to happiness was getting a job and buying a home.

Note: I'm working on a future *CPA Gone Mad* newsletter article that may change your thought process on home ownership. It will cover investment homes vs. consumption homes.

Government pushed banks to lend more money to people to buy homes. Soon banks began lending money to people who had low credit scores. Then the banks let individuals borrow more than they could afford by structuring variable interest rate loans. They also didn't require detailed financial records and used all sorts of borderline sketchy methods.

Why would banks do this? First, the laws encouraged it. Second, their job is to make money, not to do the right thing for you. The more loans banks initiate, the more they get in fees. And banks didn't keep most of these loans. They sold them in packages on Wall Street.

Before this bust that occurred, since World War II, housing had always gone up. Everyone assumed housing would always continue to go up. This belief contributed to these riskier loans.

These new loans to people who could not afford them (subprime) created a bubble. As people with low credit scores could afford higher priced houses, housing prices kept going up. Risky loans created more hungry buyers.

More buyers created more demand. This drove housing prices up and up. As the value of your home increased, you felt wealthier. You were able to take out home equity loans to buy a second home, creating even more buyers. Or to buy stocks which were going up, or just to buy more things which ultimately drove stocks higher (by companies increasing earnings through selling more goods).

Banks were making so much money initiating all these loans and selling them off to Wall Street, they wanted to do more. And since housing was sky-rocketing, Wall Street was making a fortune off of the packaged loans they bought, and they demanded more.

This led banks to lower their lending standards even more. Banks were happy to do this because they sold off the loans so they seldom carried the risk. And even if they held the loans, they saw housing rising so quickly, they assumed if the loan defaulted they could immediately sell the house and cover the loans.

People began to pay more and more for homes, just to get them. They worried if they didn't buy now, they'd miss out. As we mentioned earlier, greed leads to this mentality.

It's natural. You see things going up and up. Banks encourage borrowing whatever it costs to get a home. Your financial advisors and mainstream news talk about how everyone should buy a home. People are making fortunes flipping homes. Even reading this, can you feel the urgency to profit and the worry that you might miss out? That's your fear and greed kicking in.

Remember those thoughts, feelings, and emotions. This is what the 99% thought, felt, and did. When you see something like this in the future, be skeptical.

If everyone is buying a home— even people with poor credit who can't afford the home. If people who know nothing about houses are now becoming millionaires by flipping houses, doesn't that mean everyone is "in" and we're running out of buyers?

If the 99% are buying homes, shouldn't you see this in the future? Won't you now understand that to break ahead you need to not do what everyone else is doing?

The answer is yes. This is the truth the 1% saw in 2007-2009. And those 1% made a fortune while most of the 99% lost a fortune. Did you see the movie or read the book, *The Big Short*? It's based on how a few people made a killing by shorting the housing industry.

They lost some money along the way because bubbles can go higher than anyone imagines but they knew they were right and stuck to their guns. Even though everyone told them they were crazy. The people who thought they were crazy lost a fortune. But those few that understood we had no more buyers and that the buyers who were buying were buying more than they could afford, made a small fortune.

One of the main characters, Dr. Michael Burry's fund, made his investors $750M in 2007 alone. Cornwell Capital, one of the other funds featured in *The Big Short* made more than $80M from a million-dollar bet.

You may think, it's *easy to see this looking back. But at the time it's difficult.* I agree it's difficult to see it at the time. But not because we're unable to see what's happening and know that it's going to crash.

It's difficult because the 99%, your financial advisors, mainstream media, and everyone you talk to is so convinced it's the easiest way to a fortune that if you say the opposite you're considered crazy or stupid.

Let's break down what happened. "Smart" investors, or the 1%, have formulas and strategies for valuing homes. They will not buy unless the investment fits their formula. They are very disciplined (the 99% are not). Yes, these investors had a ton of real estate during this trend.

But once the 99%, and especially the individuals with low credit or people buying more than they could afford, started driving prices up, these 1% stopped buying. The valuations on homes according to their models didn't make financial sense.

And remember the 1% has the most money so once they stopped investing; big money came out of buying. Once their money came out, home prices began to rise slower. As home prices stopped rising as fast, the individuals flipping homes or taking out home equity lines of credit didn't have access to as much capital to buy more homes.

This caused home prices to stabilize or stop rising.

Then home owners who overpaid or had low credit scores couldn't make their mortgage payments. Why? They had variable interest rate loans. Once the fixed period ended, they couldn't refinance because the price stopped rising. Interest rates, and hence mortgage payments, increased beyond what they could afford.

They began defaulting. This caused an increase in supply. Their homes were then available for sale… but the former homeowners could no longer be buyers, so the demand for home buying began to decrease. Prices started to drop. Banks couldn't get rid of these foreclosed homes because demand was no longer there.

This created a snowball effect of an increasing supply of homes. People were coming out of homes (foreclosures) and home builders (blinded by greed) were committed to huge quantities of homes that were coming onto the market. Home builders were trying to keep up with the demand. And they can't build homes overnight. So they were committed to these new homes before demand began falling. They needed to finish what they started.

Supply had now increased greatly.

And now that there were no buyers left as people realized they could not afford to buy a home, demand crashed. This led to a crash in price.

This is how the housing crash occurred….

It confirms what I have said: things get expensive, fueled by greed, and the 99% cannot believe they'll ever drop. And then things get cheap, which is typically fueled by fear, and the 99% cannot understand how they'll ever go up again.

But if you think differently and have an open mind, you can understand why things do drop. Extremes are not natural, and typically homes and other commodities return to their average price.

Bill Bonner, founder of the largest independent financial publisher has a saying "reversion to the mean….Normal exists because things tend to follow certain familiar patterns, shapes, and routines….Occasionally, of course, odd things happen. And sometimes, things change in a fundamental way. But, usually, when people say 'this time is different'…it's time to bet on normal."[2]

Mr. Bonner's February 2016 issue of his *The Bill Bonner Letter* further explains mean reversion. "Mean reversion is one of the most powerful forces in the financial markets…mean reversion is a contrarian investment strategy that refers to the tendency of stock prices to always return to a 'normal' level after reaching extreme highs or lows."

In 2009, housing became extremely cheap. You could find prime real estate available in Miami and other Florida Beach towns, California (which never happens), Arizona, Nevada, and all over the country for fractions of what it cost just 3 years before.

We had an incredible opportunity to buy prime real estate. We could have made a fortune in rent and in capital appreciation over the next years. But I didn't buy any and you probably didn't either. Why? We were afraid, and we were not prepared.

You know who did? The 1%. The owners of all the financial newsletters I subscribe to were buying prime real estate to rent out for income, and then in short time could sell for large gains. Private equity funds, which have capital from the 1%, began scooping up tons of single family homes and getting into the rental property business.

This is how you have to think differently. When assets are expensive, you need to begin raising capital so that when they become cheap you're able to scoop them up. Because when assets become cheap, as in the housing crisis, the credit markets can dry up making it impossible to get a loan.

_____

2 The Bill Bonner Letter. February 2016. Volume 3, Issue 2. "The Trade of the Century."

The 99% buy high and sell low. Think about that. Does that make any sense? You're guaranteed to lose money if you do that. They don't do it because they're stupid. They do it because the emotions of greed and fear are strong in human beings. And on top of that, the mainstream financial advisors and news outlets play into these emotions making it even harder to break free from them.

The 1% buy low and sell high. That's what you need to begin doing.

Warren Buffet has a widely popular quote "be fearful when others are greedy and greedy when others are fearful." And Rick Rule, considered one of the best natural resource investors, has said "When it comes to investing in natural resources, you're either a contrarian or you're a victim."[3]

You need to think contrarian. Over-allocate in the short term to the cheapest asset, based upon your long term asset allocation strategy you developed through the *Let Your Asset Allocation Build* model. And as assets become expensive you sell off, almost under allocating, until you get close to your long term retirement capital goal. You do this because you want to raise the capital off expensive assets to be ready to deploy in the cheap assets.

This is how you get ahead and give yourself a chance to break free from everyone else.

Now that you understand how markets cycle through highs and lows, you are prepared to think and act differently than the people who follow mainstream media. You can set yourself up to protect, profit, and prosper.

One last comment on the housing crash.

The housing crash hurt you and me. We owned homes, had a little money in our 401(k) that dropped significantly, and saw the economy experience

---

3 Jeff Clark. Growth Stock Wire. May 3, 2011. "Why It's a Bad Time to Buy Oil Stocks Right Now."

a crash which made it hard for people to recover. But we worked hard, began saving money, and are now back on track. We're learning from it and preparing how to protect and profit from the next big crash.

That's why I wrote this book and why you're reading it.

But we need to look at the other piece of the housing crash. The one that really caused the economy to suffer, the stock market to crash, and the situation we're in today. Housing was the trigger but not the root cause.

Chapter 3

Fallout from the Last Financial Crisis

How government intervention hurt the average person, helped the already wealthy, and set us up for another crisis

The financial crisis of 2007-2009 was more than just housing. If you watched or read *The Big Short*, you may already understand this. But it's so important to the overall thesis of this book that we must discuss it.

Housing triggered the crisis but it was not the root of all the pain that was caused. As I mentioned, it hurt you and me but it would not have had the lasting, devastating, comprehensive impact if it was just housing.

There was another side to the housing crash that led to it being termed a financial crisis.

Banks, Wall Street, and Credit created the crisis and were not allowed to self-correct

If you recall, Lehman Brothers, a giant investment bank, went bankrupt out of the financial crisis. This was triggered by the housing crisis, but what caused them to go bankrupt was their amount of leverage.

Leverage is basically using credit to invest. You and I need to save money in order to invest. Investment banks borrow money and invest this borrowed money. That is how they make such huge returns on their capital.

They take a little capital, borrow money against it and now have much more capital to invest. This allows them to maximize gains. The problem with leverage is it also maximizes losses.

What was Lehman Brothers investing in with leverage that caused them to collapse? Financial instruments that were based upon packaged mortgages. Remember in the last chapter we said that banks would package these loans given to people with low credit scores and for more than they could afford. Then they would sell them on Wall Street.

Since housing was going up so fast, Wall Street was making a fortune buying and selling these packaged loans. And because they believed it would continue, they were using really large amounts of borrowed money to buy and sell these loans.

How the Bubble Burst

When these loans began to go bad, just like we explained in the housing market itself, not only do the prices drop but everyone begins to sell out of fear. This fear and selling panic drives prices lower and lower.

If you invested with your own money, you lost your own money. But when you invested with borrowed money, you not only lost your own money, you also lost someone else's money. Lehman Brothers lost all of its money and could not repay its borrowed money causing it to fail.

Lehman Brothers went bankrupt but the problem wasn't isolated. All the banks that lent Lehman Brothers this money now had loans to Lehman

Brothers that would never be repaid. These banks suffered drastic losses because they had to write off these loans.

And Lehman Brothers wasn't the only firm doing this, they were the only big name you hear about failing. Other firms lost tons of money and borrowed capital causing the housing crash to create a crisis throughout the whole financial industry. This is why it was termed the financial crisis or credit crisis.

It didn't stop there. General Motors, who we all know of as a car manufacturer, has a lending arm as well—GMAC. This arm, which had been one of the most profitable parts of GM prior to the crisis, went bankrupt. Then, when you factor in people losing a bunch of their "wealth" as home equity evaporated or they lost their homes and suddenly nobody could buy cars.

This caused GM to go bankrupt. When GM goes bankrupt and is one of the largest manufacturers in the US buying parts from many US suppliers, all those suppliers suffer and go bankrupt.

Nothing is isolated. The economy is connected. So when greed drives up prices, the economy becomes dependent upon it staying that way. But as we explained earlier, when things get expensive and there are no buyers left, the price can only go one direction. **Down.**

When it begins to go down, fear drives it down fast. And since the connected economy sucked in profits when it was going higher, the whole economy begins to suffer and almost fail when it begins to dive lower.

I truly believe the financial crisis of 2007-2008 should have been much worse than it was. I thought a massive depression was coming and it was going to be terrible. But there is one force that always attempts to stop a massive depression and suffering economy from happening….

The Government Steps In

Before I explain what it is, I have to make a disclaimer because I don't want people to stop reading. This is not a political book. Personally, I'm a libertarian. I'm not trying to say that what happened next was right or wrong. As a libertarian, I believe government has a very limited role which is to provide national defense and protection of its citizens and to enforce personal property laws. And by protection of its citizens, I mean from someone else causing direct personal harm. Very limited.

What I'm about to say is not casting blame on any political party, I just want to explain what happened so you can understand the situation we're in today and the opportunities we have to protect and profit in the very near future.

Lehman Brothers went bankrupt. GM was bailed out by the US government. Many other banks were also bailed out by the government. AIG, a large insurance company, was saved by the government. Why was Lehman Brothers allowed to fail and many other Wall Street institutions were not? I have no idea. I just want to explain why not allowing these institutions to fail (regardless of whether you think they should have or not) created the situation we're in today.

Did government intervention stop the financial crisis from having a much worse impact on the economy and individuals like you and me? Most likely it did in the short term. If the government would have just let these businesses fail, the short term effects probably would have been much worse.

But if the bad business practices, over borrowing, and risky lending would have failed; most likely things would have gotten better, quicker. This is all speculation but when you prop something up by government intervention, you are just pushing the inevitable down the road.

You don't need to agree with any of the last two paragraphs. It's basically irrelevant to the message. The key of all of this; when you stop these bad business practices, over borrowing, and risky lending from failing; **people do not experience the true consequences of their behavior!**

We could debate forever on whether the government intervention was good or bad. But where we must agree is that by intervening, it created a false sense of security for the Wall Street firms, investment bankers, and businesses that were taking on too much risk. It created an environment in which they do not suffer from the consequences of their behavior. That is what created the environment we're in today.

I just want to make sure you understand how we need to agree on that. You and I got hurt by the financial crisis and experienced pain for buying into high home prices and chasing big stock gains. But the individuals who created the bubble and subsequent crash by touting the financial ideas, risky lending, and overextending their borrowing did not (other than Lehman Brothers). If it doesn't hurt, often you don't learn.

Now that we agree on that key point and agree that we don't need to determine whether the government intervention was good or bad, let's discuss what the government intervention entailed and how they stopped the financial crisis from being worse and created the "recovery" (more in Chapter 4 on the "recovery") we have experienced in the years since.

The US is the world's largest economy with China right behind. When the US economy suffers a financial crisis, like back in 2008, it is not contained within the US. Remember how we explained how connected the economy is within the US? Well, the world economy is just as connected.

We buy goods from other countries. We sell goods and services to other countries. The big banks have investment and banking practices in multiple countries. So when the largest economy in the World suffers a financial crisis, the entire World suffers since we are connected through Global Trade.

Weapon #1. Lower Interest Rates

One of the biggest weapons the government has to prevent a depression and to stop a financial crisis is to lower interest rates. Lower interest rates, theoretically, entice people to borrow and spend money. When money is being spent, it flows through the economy multiple times creating increased economic output.

For example, if I borrow $100k to buy a house, that does not just have the impact of giving the sellers of the house a $100k. The sellers of the house may be using that $100k to buy a brand new house. So the home builder takes that $100k to pay the workers and buy materials. The workers then use the money to buy food and pay for services they use. The companies that make the materials use it to pay their workers who buy food and pay for services they use.

The grocery store gets the money from people buying food and pays their employees and so on and so on.

That is the idea behind the government using lower interest rates against a depression or a recession. It's their way to get the economy going. Lower interest rates encourage borrowing and subsequent spending which filters through the entire economy.

Lower interest rates also mean you are paid less to save your money. If you are paid less to save your money, the idea is that you will spend it. This would then have the same positive results in the economy as just discussed.

Lower interest rates have another effect as well. Lower interest rates weaken the currency of the country with the lower interest rates. We'll get more into this later but want to touch on it briefly here.

If interest rates are lower in the US, this means you are paid less money to save US dollars. If holding US dollars earns you less interest, then investors move money out of the US dollar and into other currencies which pay higher interest. This may not be what you and I do but it's what the 1% and other wealthy investors do.

They may move their money to another currency or to safe bonds. Either way, this makes our currency "weaker" because lower interest reduces demand for the currency.

When you have a weaker US dollar it makes goods and services produced in the US cheaper for foreign buyers. Again, the hope is it will cause foreign buyers to purchase more US goods and services to stimulate the US economy. Since the world suffers when the US suffers, a strong US economy is good for the world.

This all led to what is called Zero Interest Rate Policy (ZIRP). ZIRP is creating low or almost zero interest to stimulate borrowing and spending. As I mentioned, this is the government's top defense to stop a recession and depression to stimulate the economy.

When I say government, I mean the government economists at the Federal Reserve. Government economists work with numbers and averages. But they don't understand what real people like you and me are actually facing in their world. Bill Bonner wrote a great book on this titled *Hormegeddon*.

One of the best examples I remember from the book is something to this effect. Let's say you make $200k per year, are married, have 2 kids, 2 cars, and spend $20k per year on medical costs. I on the other hand make $100k per year, am single, have no kids, 1 car, and spend practically nothing per year on medical costs.

This is a simple, exaggerated example, but this is really how government economists operate. They don't know or understand my personal situation, wants, needs, and values. They don't know your personal situation, wants, needs, and values. They just have the above data about both of us.

Government economists, and ultimately the politicians, see this data and say, "The average person in the US makes $150k per year, is half married, has 1 kid, 1.5 cars, and spends $10k per year on medical costs." Then they develop plans and ideas to help that average person.

I don't make $150k per year. You don't have just 1 kid or spend only $10k on medical costs. Neither of us are half married. If they're helping that average person, they're not helping either one of us in that data pool. You may think I'm exaggerating and making fun of the government but this is honestly how they think.

They sit in their bubble and just work with the data they have and try to help that *average* person. They don't actually know you or me and what's good for either of us. Read Bill Bonner's book for how this creates issues across all areas of government intervention.

So when the government intervenes with low interest rates, with the intention of helping you and me, they are actually helping someone who doesn't exist. **This creates unintended consequences.**

When government intervened with the good intention of stopping a huge depression by bailing out GM, the banks, and Freddie Mac/Fannie Mae, they created the unintended consequences of bad behavior not punished by true consequences. ZIRP did the same thing.

After the financial crisis, most of America (you and me) had no cash. Our credit was hurt. We were underwater on our homes and had no home equity. Some of us lost jobs. We were stunned by sinking housing values. We'd never seen it before.

Most of us were unable to borrow money with the low interest rates. Our credit was weak and we had no assets or no job. Even if we were able to borrow money, we didn't want to. We were not going to borrow for a house because we were scared. All we wanted to do was try and save money. But we couldn't even do that because interest rates were so low.

These low interest rates didn't encourage us to spend our money. Instead, it led us to save even more money to make up for the low interest rates. We had to save even more just to get to what we could have saved when interest rates were higher.

On top of that, banks didn't want to lend to us. They were just on the verge of bankruptcy from lending too much to you and me. Yes, they were bailed out by the government, but they were still working to get their business back on solid ground. The last thing they wanted to do was give out a loan that paid them almost zero interest for the risk they were undertaking.

So while the low interest rates made sense to the government economists sitting around a table with their numbers, it didn't make sense to us or the banks. It didn't do what it was intended

Weapon #2. Quantitative Easing– QE

When these low interest rate policies didn't get the economy going, the Feds tried QE. QE is basically the government creating more US dollars to push into the economy. The idea here is that the government pushes more money into the economy hoping people stimulate the economy by borrowing and spending.

This was mostly accomplished as the US government printed money and used it to buy bonds. Theoretically this creates more liquidity in the bond markets. Again, this liquidity is meant to indirectly put more money into the economy so it can grow.

The government doesn't literally "print" more US dollars. We are basically turning into a cashless society where everything financial is done through data on computers. The government just creates more money on their balance sheet and then buys these bonds.

When the government purchases these bonds, it puts more liquidity— or money— in the credit market. More available money allows investments by companies and wealthy individuals. It doesn't directly go to you and me who were hurt the most and need the most help.

I'll admit; QE helped a little. But it was nowhere near a 1 for 1 impact. $1 dollar of QE did not create $1 dollar of economic increase. Why? The same reasons as above. The government economists are just working with data on what the average "whatever" should do. But it's not what everyone did do.

A lot of big corporations had their stock price drop dramatically during the financial crisis. As banks, investment firms, and individuals began losing money due to the housing crisis, people began selling stocks. As stocks started to drop, fear set in and this led to more and more selling.

Good companies found their stocks at yard sale prices in 2009. Steve Sjuggerud, who has a Ph.D. in finance and writes several newsletters for Stansberry Research, told how he took out home equity loans to buy stocks at a price far below their true value. When they bounced back... he made a ton of money.

Many large corporations know exactly what their stock is "worth." When it became extremely cheap, they didn't use QE and ZIRP to increase their spending on growing their business which would stimulate the economy as the government intended. They used this liquidity created by QE to borrow money to buy their own stock.

We'll get into this shortly as we discuss the "recovery" but we need to take our first break.

INTERLUDE 1: Key Economic and Financial Terms Explained

This book is intended for those who are not in the 1% and are not finance and investing professionals. It is written to explain wealth building simply and easily to hard working Americans who want a chance to get ahead. You need to know how to get ahead without paying a fortune to some mainstream financial advisor who is not operating in your best interest.

This book is written to give you the tools to feel confident about investing your retirement funds to get ahead. That way you can focus on what you do best and enjoy doing most.

That being said, finance and investing can be confusing, and not all terminology is understood the same way by everyone. We've already addressed a lot and I've tried to explain terms along the way. But before moving forward and explaining the situation we're in today and the incredible opportunity that exists, I want to take some time to explain some key financial and investing concepts.

This is a guide you can easily refer back to. Hopefully it will clarify any confusion and assist in your understanding as we go forward.

Stock Valuations: Stocks are typically valued by most analysts based on a multiple of earnings per share. The multiple varies by industry and by type of company (growth, value, dividend paying). If an individual company earned $10 per share and it was valued at a multiple of 15 you would expect to pay $150 per share. I'm not suggesting you should use this as your only method of valuing stocks. I'm explaining this is how most analysts look at stock valuations.

Earnings per Share: Another way to value a stock is based on the earnings per share. This is a company's net income (or earnings) divided by number of shares held by investors. You may hear terminology such as "adjusted earnings per share" which basically mean certain things were adjusted out of net income before dividing by the total number of shares. To summarize: Numerator is Net Income (earnings) and Denominator is Shares outstanding.

Stock Buyback: A stock buyback, which was briefly introduced at the end of the previous chapter, is when a company buys its own stock. What this means is they use cash on hand or borrowed cash to purchase outstanding shares. This has the effect of reducing shares outstanding (in terms of earnings per share, it reduces the denominator) so it makes that multiple look better. If you own the stock and the company buys back shares, it has the effect of increasing your ownership in the company. This can be great for investors if the company has plenty of cash and buys when shares are undervalued because you then own more of the company without buying more shares yourself. It can be bad if the company incurs debt and buys shares when they are overvalued.

Dividends: These are payments companies make to shareholders. Typically, these are paid quarterly and, in some instances, one-time special dividends are paid. Dividends divided by the company's current stock price is considered the dividend yield. If you are able to purchase a solid, long-term, dividend-paying stock at a great price (such as Coke mentioned earlier) you can collect a very nice income stream. Especially when the company consistently raises its dividend. If the company raises its dividend, your personal dividend yield increases because the numerator (dividend payout) increases while the denominator (your stock purchase price) stays the same.

Listed (or nominal) Price: This is the quoted value of a stock, or any investment for that matter. If a stock has a low nominal price ($2) it does not mean it's "cheap" compared to a stock that has a high nominal price ($500). The $500 stock could be much cheaper than the $2 stock. Please make sure you understand this before buying any stocks. The same goes for rental real estate. A $100k house in rural West Virginia may be much more expensive than a $400k smaller house near the coast in California. In order to determine if a stock is cheap, you typically look at a multiple of Free Cash Flow, Earnings per Share, and Book Value. Once you value the company based on those metrics, you compare it to the nominal price to determine if it is cheap. Remember, a low nominal price does not mean cheap. A high nominal price does not mean expensive.

Free Cash Flow: This is a great measure of a company's health. It's the cash a company earns from operating its business, less its operating expenses and capital expenditures. If a company can generate consistent positive cash flow after reinvesting in its business through capital expenditures I get interested in the company. But that alone does not mean the company is a buy. It could be valued at too high of a multiple to warrant buying today. You can think of rental real estate in these terms too. If you generate operating cash from your rental property and spend little in expenses (mortgage, insurance, taxes, repairs), you would generate free cash flow.

Capital Expenditure: This is a company's reinvestment in its business. A capital expenditure is considered spending to create an asset that will deliver a return in excess of its cost for more than one year. Some companies must continue to spend on capital expenditures in order to generate income and cash flow. That's why subtracting capital expenses from operating income to get free cash flow is a great measure of a company's health. If a company generates cash flow from operating but has to spend substantially more than that amount on capital expenditures each year, that's normally not a good sign.

Book Value: This is a company's assets minus its liabilities. Lots of times analysts will look at book value per share. This is just book value divided by shares outstanding.

Fixed Income: Fixed income is typically considered a bond or government debt. Anything that pays a fixed amount of income (i.e. fixed interest rate) for a specific time period is considered fixed income.

Assets: Assets are anything expected to deliver a return (pay you) over its life above its current value. Assets can be land. Assets can be other businesses. Assets can be loans you've made that, over time, will earn you more than what you loaned out. Art, stocks, mineral rights, homes. As long as what you expect to receive for that asset in value or cash is greater than its cost, it's an asset.

Liabilities: The opposite of assets. These are things that cost you money to have or operate. Obligations you must meet.

Credit: Credit is borrowed money. I like to think of credit as money borrowed for a short time period— like your credit card. You can also think of credit as having the access or right to borrow money. You may not have officially borrowed money, but if that money is available to you, that can be thought of as access to credit.

Debt: Debt is borrowed money. I typically think of debt as money borrowed for a longer period of time— like your 30 year mortgage. A short term purchase on a credit card that will be paid back in 30 days, I consider credit. This is not a hard rule, but I think of debt as being larger amounts of money than credit as well. This is because larger amounts are typically borrowed for longer periods and smaller amounts are typically borrowed for shorter periods. But obviously the size depends upon the borrower's ability to obtain credit.

Commodity: Commodities are something that is typically considered naturally available in the world. In other words, it's not something special that someone creates. Commodities are typically thought of in terms of copper, iron ore, oil, nickel, natural gas, corn, pigs, etc. I also think of houses as a commodity sometimes. Precious metals such as gold, silver, or platinum can also be considered commodities. The main difference is they are much rarer.

Commodity Cycles: Commodities, as described above, go through price cycles. The reason this occurs is because they have to be mined, grown and harvested, drilled, born and raised, etc. If the supply of a commodity exceeds the demand, the price drops. Most producers can't sit on the commodities they produce because they need the cash to continue to produce more of the commodity. So when the supply exceeds demand, they still need to sell what they have, but since there is an oversupply the price drops.

When the price is low, they don't produce as much because it's not very profitable for them. When demand begins to exceed supply, prices begin to rise very quickly. This is because you cannot just magically produce commodities overnight. If you began cutting back on production when prices were low since you were earning little cash, it will take you time to get production levels up to the new demand. This is because you have to grow, raise, explore, drill, and mine the commodity, which takes several years. In the meantime, prices rise quickly.

With this excess cash you invest in more and more production to meet demand. Then when demand drops below supply again, all the excess production created by the excess cash keeps supply high for a while. This is because you typically have production that keeps producing. You can't shut it off immediately. Calves must grow up; wheat fields must grow to harvest. This drives prices down again. And so the cycles continue. This happens with all commodities and, if you understand them, you can make a lot of money. Think T. Boone Pickens.

Insurance: Most people have insurance but they don't really understand insurance. Insurance is protection. You don't buy it because you expect something to happen. Or even because you hope something will happen. You buy it to protect yourself from what you hope will be the unlikely instance something bad does happen. You cannot know what other people will do or what environment will present itself down the road, so you protect yourself.

You buy car insurance not because you plan to get in a car accident or hope you get in a car accident. You buy it so you're protected if you happen to get into a car accident. Most likely because someone else causes the car accident!

Same with life insurance. You don't buy it because you expect or hope to die soon. You buy it because the world is uncertain, people do strange things, and you could be in a situation where you happen to die.

Homeowners insurance is the same. You take care of your home and expect and hope it's always in good shape. But what if someone else breaks in, a tornado hits, or hail damages your roof. You want to be protected.

People think I'm crazy when I say this but I consider a prenuptial agreement to be insurance. You're not entering into one because you hope or even expect to get divorced but people are always changing and the environment around us causes us to change. So, in the unlikely event that one of you decides sometime down the road to no longer be married, a prenuptial agreement can provide protection or insurance.

Insurance is protection. Not something you buy because of expecting or hoping something will occur but to protect you in the event something does happen. Life is unpredictable. Protect yourself.

Currency: A currency is anything used to perform trade within an economy. The US dollar is the currency we use in America. If I want to buy or sell something, I do it with US dollars. Bitcoin is becoming a currency. People use bitcoin to buy and sell goods or services. All goods and services are assigned a value based on this currency. For example, I might price my riding mower for $600 in America's currency.

Exchange Rate: An exchange rate is the rate at which two different currencies are exchanged. I like to think of it as the price you pay for one currency in terms of another currency. Currencies are continually in flux, with one rising or falling against the other. At one point US/Canadian dollars were nearly 1:1. At another time, one Canadian dollar could only buy .75 USD.

Above we explained how US dollars and Bitcoin are both operating as currencies. Let's say the business that sold me the riding mower doesn't want to accept US dollars and only wants to accept Bitcoin. I would need to exchange my US dollars for Bitcoin in order to make the purchase. How many bitcoins could I get for my 600 US dollars depends upon the dollar price of Bitcoin (or exchange rate).

To simplify let's say the exchange rate is 600 US dollars for 1 Bitcoin. This means the US dollar price for 1 Bitcoin is 600. I would give someone 600 US dollars and they would give me 1 Bitcoin. The business then says the Bitcoin price of the lawnmower is 1 Bitcoin and I exchange the Bitcoin for the lawnmower. If that business now wants to pay his employees and he must pay his employees in US dollars, he must exchange that 1 Bitcoin for US dollars.

Inflation/Deflation: Inflation is when the purchasing power of your money goes down. In other words, when your money (US dollars for most of us) purchases less of what it used to. Deflation is when the purchasing power of your money goes up. In other words, when your money (US dollars again) purchase more than what it used to. How does this happen?

In a simple example, you have a set amount of US dollars. The price (or exchange rate) of those US dollars would be based on the production of the US economy. If the US economy is producing well, those dollars become more valuable. The same amount of US dollars in a growing economy would allow that same amount of US dollars to buy more of what is now available (deflation).

If the US economy is decreasing or regressing, those dollars become worth less. The same amount of US dollars in a shrinking economy would allow that same amount of US dollars to buy less of what is now available (inflation).

Here's another way to think of it. If we have a static economy that is neither growing nor shrinking, your money should keep the same value— neither inflating nor deflating. If we reduce the amount of money available, your money compared to the economy would be worth more. You'd be able to buy more than what you could before due to deflation. If we add to the amount of money available, your money compared to the economy would be worth less. You'd be able to buy less than what you could before due to inflation.

* If money available goes up faster than the economy: inflation.
* If it goes down faster than the economy: deflation.
* If the economy goes up faster than money supply: deflation.
* If the economy goes down faster than money supply: inflation.

Strong Currency: When there's more demand for a currency such as US dollars this is typically due to the economy rising faster than the money supply. The demand for the currency typically comes from foreign countries who want to buy our goods. Remember, goods in the US are priced in US dollars. If our economy is growing and countries want to buy our goods, they need more US dollars. If we do not increase our money supply to stay consistent with the rising economy, that creates deflation for the US currency. Our currency can buy more goods than what it previously could. This is considered a strong currency.

Weak Currency: When there is less demand for a currency such as US dollars, this is typically due to an economy shrinking faster than the money supply. The lower demand is typically due to foreign countries who do NOT want to buy our goods. If our economy is shrinking and countries do not want to buy our goods, they need less US dollars. If we do not shrink our money supply to stay consistent with the shrinking economy, that creates inflation for the US currency. Our currency can buy fewer goods than what it previously could. This is considered a weak currency.

Connected World Economy: In the examples above, we were looking at very simple and isolated examples. But remember the entire world economy is connected and you cannot judge one country in a vacuum. If the US dollar is increasing in supply faster than its economy, that can create inflation for the US dollar. But you cannot assume that means a weak currency. You always have to ask *compared to what?*

If you are comparing the US dollar to the Japanese Yen, their money supply could be increasing at a faster rate compared to their economy than in the US. This means they have higher inflation in the Yen than America does in the US dollar. So even though our currency could be inflating, it may be stronger than the Yen. It's best to think of things in simple isolated terms first. But when you hear certain terminology thrown around, make sure you understand what it's being compared to.

Hopefully the explanations above gave better context to everything we previously discussed and will prepare for the next section. Read these a few times and don't hesitate to provide feedback to me if something is not clear. I will answer questions and try to clarify in my weekly newsletter. To understand what is going on today and the amazing opportunity that exists for us to get ahead and to protect ourselves from what could occur, understanding the terminology above is important.

I'll continue to reiterate some of the more complex ideas, especially when it comes to explaining the connected world economy, as we continue.

Chapter 4

The False Recovery

Learn how the "recovery" actually created a backwards functioning connected world economy

Now that we've gone over some important financial, investment, and economic concepts and terminology, let's recap where we are in our assessment of how we can position ourselves to profit from the situation that's been created.

1. We've discussed how markets go up and markets go down. And how investments and assets become expensive and cheap. We've covered how people's fear and greed is reinforced by the mainstream media and financial outlets that don't value your financial future above their own best interests.
2. We want to build towards a long term asset allocation by buying asset classes when they are cheap. Even if it means going overweight in the short term. We do this because we're not yet wealthy and are trying to build wealth in the most efficient manner possible.
3. We've talked about how understanding this and learning to think like the 1%— even though it's lonely and different than what everyone else thinks and does— is our way to get ahead.

4. We covered the cause of the boom in housing prices and subsequent housing crash and how it affected us. And how the over-leveraging of Wall Street firms multiplied the effects of the housing crash.
5. We reviewed how the economy is connected and that when one crisis begins it filters into all aspects of the economy. How when the government intervened it didn't allow the corporations and individuals who were exhibiting bad behavior to feel the pain. The pain was felt by you and me who were only doing what the media and financial outlets suggested.
6. Then we discussed the "tools" the government used to prevent a massive depression and get us out of the recession. And how the government economists do what's best based on data but it doesn't actually represent what you and I will do.
7. We learned why the Feds deployed ZIRP and QE and why they failed. And because the government economists think about tools in terms of data and not reality, there are unintended consequences. We ended by beginning to talk about the "recovery."

The problem? There really wasn't a recovery.

If you watch mainstream media and get financial advice through typical outlets, you probably hear a lot about how much the economy has "recovered" since 2009.

Have You Felt the "Recovery"?

But the "recovery" you hear about is all relative. It's due to the massive amounts of government debt added around the world. Yes, certain things have recovered but has your personal situation recovered? Hopefully you have a good paying job. Hopefully your income has gone up. But do you have more savings than you had in 2007? Do you have more investments than you did in 2007? Is your standard of living as good as it was in 2007?

I honestly hope the answer to all of these is yes. And if it is, most likely it's because you're a hard working American in the right situation during your peak earning years. If you are 30-40 years old today which I am, you were 20-30 years old back in 2007.

When I was 20-30, I didn't have any money saved as I was just starting out in my career, paying off my student loans, getting my first new car (which I still drive today), and overpaying for a house I thought I needed to own.

I didn't lose my job during the financial crisis because I was in an industry (accounting) where you're needed through all cycles. I hope you're in the same boat.

Fast forward 9-10 years and I have substantially more savings, substantially more investments, earn substantially more, almost no debt, own rental real estate, and rent my own home. If you ask me if I'm doing better today than back in 2007, the answer is absolutely yes.

Does it have anything to do with an economic recovery that was fueled by ZIRP and QE? Absolutely not.

I'm doing better today because I was in an early part of my career back in 2007 and just beginning to hit my peak earning years. I was already out of college and established in my career field. And I worked hard, saved, and learned how to get ahead. I hope you did the same. If so, kudos to you. You're better off than you were in 2007.

But don't mistake the fact you're better off for an economic recovery. Many of your fellow readers of this book are in much worse shape and haven't recovered. This book is for all of you who want to get ahead. So don't stop reading just because you were fortunate to be in a situation to get ahead during the last 9 years. It doesn't mean the economy has recovered. It doesn't guarantee you're protected from what's about to come. And it doesn't stop you from profiting from the situation we're in.

It just means you should have more capital and current earnings to protect and to profit from. But please know you are a small subset of the 99%. Most of the 99% are not doing much better.

Unemployment may be down but people are working part-time when they were working full-time. Or people are working two jobs. Or people have stopped looking for work at all.

We need to be honest with ourselves; the economy is not doing well. Fewer people are working. Companies are making less money. By the second quarter of 2016, the S&P 500 Index of companies reported five consecutive quarters of falling earnings.[4] Earnings are expected to rise in Q3/Q4 of 2016 but only by a small margin, most likely due to holiday shopping.

I think this is part of what drove Donald J. Trump's election as the next US President.

The 1% has made a fortune due to the stock market rising, bond prices rising, and assets in general going up. Mainstream media says inflation has been nowhere to be found and that the US dollar is strong. Financial news outlets keep talking about how the market just continues to grind higher.

The real middle class, including those of us not at the right point in our careers to take advantage of the 2008 crisis, is not better off. Again to take an example from *Bill Bonner's Diary*:

---

4 Justin Brill. Stansberry Digest. September 26th 2016. "The World's Most Dangerous Bank is In Trouble."

"Today's economy no longer seems to work for the average American... He had to work 990 hours to buy a Ford F-150 pickup in 1976. Forty years later, he has to put in 1,220 hours...A new Ford F-150 pickup costs upward of $26,000 today. The same basic truck was about $15,000 in 1996...Yes, that's right. It is better. More electronic gear. Airbags. And so forth...."

"But, of course, the man who needs a pickup truck cannot go to the dealer and say, 'I just want $15,000 worth of pickup. You know, like I got in 1996'... He still has to pay the full $26,000...and it still does basically the same job it did during the Clinton administration. It takes him and his tools from point A to point B. But it costs him 70% more."[5]

We're now going to bridge the disconnect between mainstream media and financial outlet news and reality.

Do Stocks and a Strong Dollar *Really* Point to a "Recovery"?

First, we'll talk about the economic recovery along with the corresponding stock market rise. Then move on to why you're told inflation doesn't exist and the US dollar is so strong. Finally we'll end this chapter with a discussion of how the 1% got extremely wealthy over the last 9-10 years. This is important because it's what we're going to use to protect ourselves and profit greatly over the next 5-10 years.

Did ZIRP and QE really create an economic recovery? I honestly don't believe so but it depends on how you look at it. I think all it did was set things up for an oncoming crisis that's even worse. ZIRP and QE flushed trillions of dollars into the economy in an attempt to stimulate it.

If you look at economist data, it suggests this had some positive impacts on the US economy. But remember we're not isolated. These "tools" created

---

5 Bill Bonner. Bill Bonner's Diary. October 12, 2016. "Who Still Supports Trump?" and Bill Bonner. Bill Bonner's Diary. October 25, 2016. "Economists Have Ruined the Economy."

a weaker US dollar. Once we had a weaker US dollar, it made US goods and services cheaper than other countries' goods and services. I'll explain this further in the next chapter on currency wars but for the time being just know: when one currency weakens another currency must strengthen.

The US was weakening it's currency against all other countries. Again, the hope was that if we stimulated the US economy it would be good for the rest of the world. So while economists may tell you we saw an improvement in the US economy, my argument is that all we did was steal market share of the world economy.

The World Bank National Accounts data, and OECD National Accounts data shows the GDP growth for the world since 2007, just before the last financial crisis:[6]

2007: 4.311%
2008: 1.85%
2009: -1.718%
2010: 4.35%
2011: 3.112&
2012: 2.465%
2013: 2.393%
2014: 2.612%
2015: 2.466%

Government economists make an argument for a growing world economy. But notice the GDP growth has basically fallen since 2010. And the world's GDP growth is nowhere near what it was before the 2008 financial crisis.

In fact, this GDP growth has been fueled by record government debt increases around the world. Take a look at the following charts that show government debt or government spending from around the world's largest economies.

---

6 The World Bank. GDP growth (annual %). http://data.worldbank.org/indicator/NY.GDP.
MKTP.KD.ZG?end=2015&start=2007&view=chart

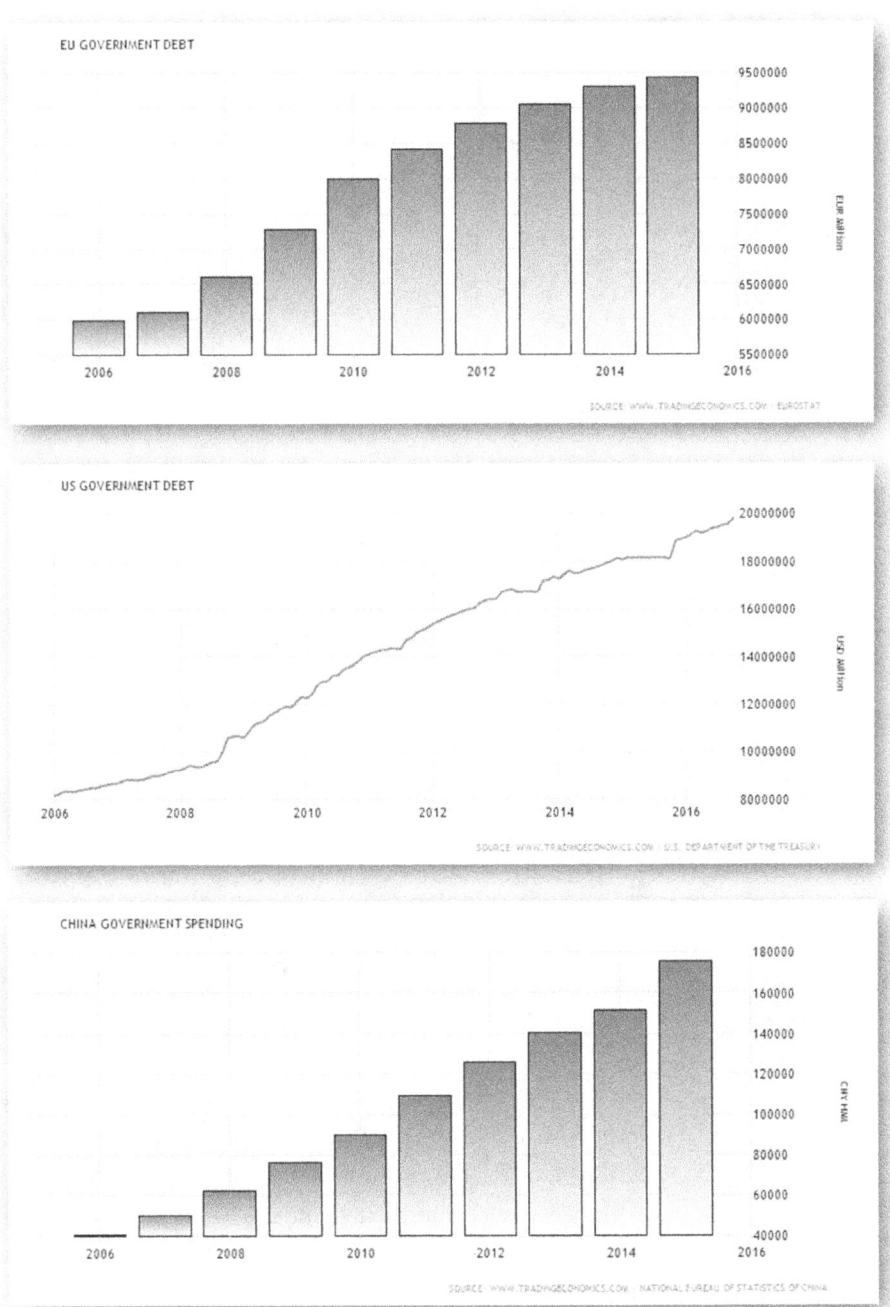

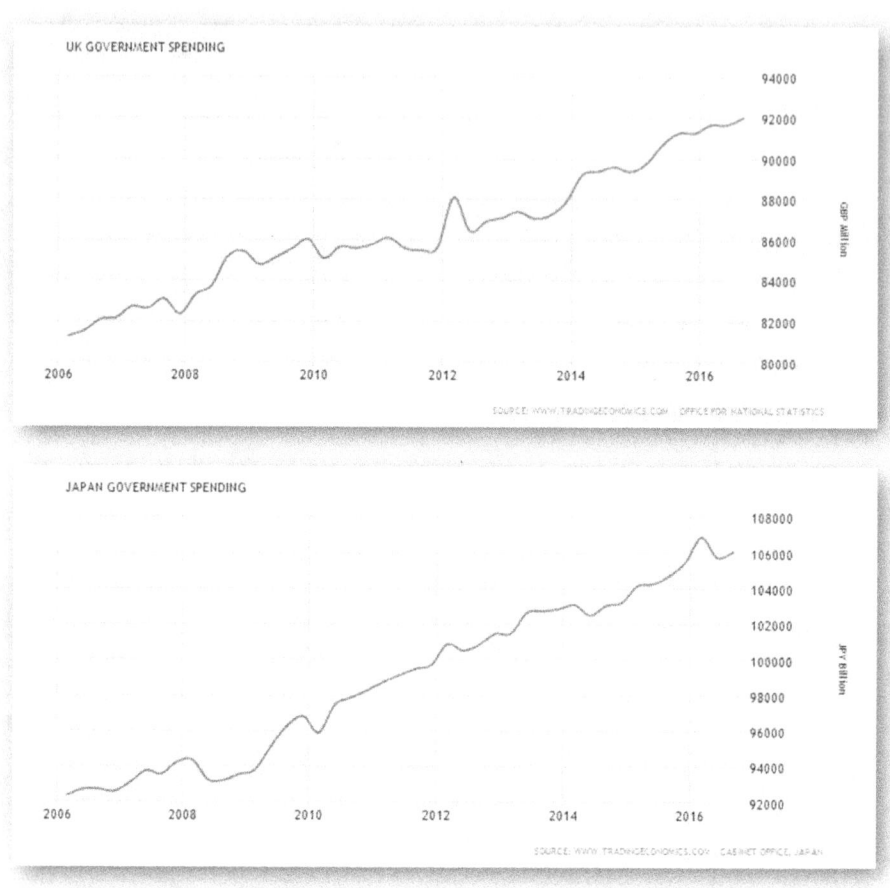

Of the world's largest economies, government debt and government spending has been rapidly increasing since the last financial crisis. The debt and spending are still increasing while World GDP growth is slowing.

This is why I argue that the government economists may have created an artificial economic recovery on the surface. But in reality they spent massive amounts of money to push the problem out into the future. They've done nothing to reduce debt (it's still increasing), and their spending has not spurred GDP.

If ZIRP and QE had improved the US economy as it was intended to, these economies wouldn't be suffering. You wouldn't see world GDP growth slowing during a period of record government debt and spending.

I believe all that occurred is the US took market share of the world economy which gave the appearance of the US economy improving while other countries' economies got worse.

You may think that this is okay because all that matters to you is what happens in the US. But the world economy is very interconnected. If we used ZIRP and QE to "kick the can down the road" by stealing market share while creating worsening economies in other countries, this will hurt America in the long run.

We previously read that earnings of the S&P 500 Index of companies dropped 5 consecutive quarters through Q2 2016. That shows a weakening US economy. So we really aren't in a strong "recovery" at all.

And just as one crisis— such as the housing crisis— is not isolated to housing alone, one crisis in one country is not isolated to that country alone. With world government debt and spending much higher than in 2007, the crisis that comes next will be much worse.

Another proof the mainstream media gives that the economy has strengthened is that the stock market has fully recovered and hit all-time highs.

True. The stock market has hit all-time highs. But remember the chart in Chapter 2? It showed the market tends to hit record highs before big corrections. The market is now extremely expensive and close to where most markets stall and begin to tailspin.

In Chapter 3 we briefly mentioned how ZIRP created extremely low, almost zero percent interest rates. And QE created additional money (liquidity) in the bond market. Companies used that cheap money to buy back stock. This has led to corporations having extremely high levels of debt.

From Porter Stansberry, founder of Stansberry Research, "U.S corporate bonds outstanding are currently worth almost $8 trillion, roughly 45% of U.S.

gross domestic product (GDP)." This is the output of the US economy in total. Stansberry continues "Corporate debt in the U.S. has consistently topped out at a little less than 45% of GDP. Historically, debt cycle has turned at that point. Defaults rise, issuance declines, and a bear market begins….This cycle is likely to be far worse than average. Thanks to the government's 2008/2009 intervention, we haven't gone through a legitimate market-clearing cycle since 2002. Bond market veterans are expecting something around $1.5 trillion in defaults through 2021 – or about three times more in defaults than we saw in the mortgage crisis."[7]

The government encouraged this additional debt hoping it would lead to investment in the economy to create growth. But it didn't. Corporations didn't invest in the economy. Corporations borrowed this cheap money in order to buy back their own stock when it was at a discounted price.

Think about this, if you borrow money for almost nothing and use it to buy back massive quantities of your stock you can cause your earnings per share (EPS) to increase **even if earnings are going down**. Remember, EPS is net income divided by shares outstanding. If shares outstanding go down at a faster pace than net income is dropping, EPS can still go up.

A company can make their stock appear more valuable even if its earnings are dropping just by borrowing money for almost nothing and buying back their stock. This shifty accounting tricks stock buyers.

Large corporations are also borrowing huge amounts of money to buy other companies at premium prices. One way to show revenue growth— if your revenue is not growing— is to buy another company and add their revenue to yours. You get revenue growth because you're able to borrow large sums of money at almost no cost.

---

7 Porter Stansberry. Stansberry Digest. September 30th, 2016. "How to Make a Fortune as $300 Billion in Corporate Debt Explodes."

On top of this, the same risky lending that crept into the housing industry in 2007 is now thriving in the auto industry. And the situation is even worse. A house is something that everyone needs. There's typically demand over the long term for housing. But a car is known to be a depreciating asset. That means it goes down in value over time and eventually becomes worth nothing. And many people don't absolutely need cars.

In 2007 banks gave loans to poor credit customers for more than they could afford. This is called subprime lending. Subprime lending is now in the auto industry. Loans are being issued to people with low credit scores. And because they can't afford the monthly payments on a typical 48 or 60 month loan, loans are being given for 84 months. Think about that. It will take you 7 years to pay off your car. I don't know may people who keep their car for 7 years. And many cars need extensive repairs prior to 7 years. As of June 30, 2016 US auto loan debt was $1.103 Trillion.[8]

In 2016 a record 32% of new car purchasers came in with a car that had an underwater loan on it. In other words, they owed more on the car than it was worth.[9] They traded it in for a new car and a debt that included both the new car and the amount they still owed on the old car!

That's not the only debt we're dealing with. Debt has filtered into the college world. Student loan debt is at all-time highs now, closing in on $1.3 Trillion.[10] Student debt grows when college graduates can't find jobs (or jobs that pay anything substantial) and when the price of college tuition skyrockets. Many students are burdened with a debt that may never be paid off in their lifetime.

---

8 Allan Smith. Huffington Post: The Blog. 9/8/16. "The US Auto Loan Debt Market is Reminiscent of the Subprime Mortgage Bubble."

9 Greg Gardner. Detroit Free Press. Nov 27, 2016. "Record number of car buyers 'upside down' on trade-ins"

10 Student Loan Hero. "A Look at the Shocking Student Loan Debt Statistics for 2016. https://studentloanhero.com/student-loan-debt-statistics/

The ZIRP and QE that created the "recovery" is simply an artificial rise in the stock market created by companies borrowing money to buy back shares to increase EPS and to buy other companies to increase revenue. Car companies only look good because they've lent money to low credit individuals for 8 years to fuel car sales. Of course, when car sales go up, those profits ripple through many aspects of the economy.

This is not a "recovery," this is worrisome.

Where Is the Inflation?

With all this extra money being introduced by the government, why aren't we seeing inflation? Why do the mainstream media and financial advisors say inflation is nowhere to be seen and you have nothing to worry about? And why do they say the dollar is getting stronger?

I've seen many statistics on consumer price inflation (CPI) and it looks like inflation has not gone up quickly. But this is very misleading. Remember, if we increase the money supply and the economy does not increase at the same rate, this creates inflation. So inflation should exist but it doesn't. Why?

CPI is based on the price of selected goods rising. Prices rise when demand exceeds supply. If money supply is increasing, the theory says that demand should rise and prices should rise.

But consumers aren't spending. Corporations are borrowing money to buy back shares and buying other companies. But they are not investing in production and growth which puts money in consumer's pockets.

Most consumers are borrowing less money personally to buy homes and other goods. The exception, of course, are the ones borrowing for cars or student loans. These do little to stimulate the economy. And when consumers borrow money for cars they can't afford, this gives them even less money to spend on goods and services.

On top of that, with little to no interest on savings, consumers are saving more than in the past. They have to just to save what they would have been able to when savings earned interest.

And remember the Ford truck cost example earlier? That suggested there actually already is inflation. Look at the cost of food, rent, or other goods you buy. Have they increased in price since 2009? Is the money you earn going farther… or not as far? Does it feel like hidden inflation to you?

ZIRP and QE haven't led to an economic recovery or to overt inflation. The money hasn't flowed to consumers. They don't feel they have additional money to spend in the economy. Most of this QE money has been used to drive up the price of stocks and other assets.

Stocks are at all-time highs. Bonds are at all-time highs. Collectibles, such as art, are at all-time highs. High-end real estate is at all-time highs. And real-estate in affluent neighborhoods such as Miami and California are getting back to really high levels.

The people benefiting from ZIRP and QE are the 1% who have access to the cheap capital. But they are not spending it, they are investing in high-end assets to protect themselves from what's about to come. The only reason we don't have inflation is because the government intervention did not do what was intended.

Instead, it created a bubble in many different asset classes. ZIRP and QE, which is basically government debt, created these bubbles. Under President

Obama the US has added $7.9 trillion in debt. And this is after President Bush added $5.8 trillion.[11]

Read that last paragraph again until you understand it. That's the beginning of seeing the current situation going on in the world economy and financial markets. This is the beginning of seeing ways for you to profit from when the bubbles pop.

The Weak "Strong" Dollar

Why do we keep hearing about a strong US dollar in the mainstream media and financial outlets? You hear this because the dollar is strong. These indicators say the dollar should be weak:

* The US economy hasn't recovered
* Government intervention created an asset bubble
* Record levels of government, corporate, auto, and student loan debt

So, why is the US dollar strong? Because it's being compared to currencies that are in much worse shape. Currencies are measured one against another. You can take an average of a basket of currencies and compare one against it as well. But when you hear the US dollar is strong, that means it's strong against other currencies.

As we said, the US is the largest economy. When it struggles, everyone else struggles. When we had a crisis in 2008, the rest of the world began to slow. Then we weakened the US dollar in order to stimulate the US economy. This made US goods and services cheaper than foreign goods and services. This made the rest of the world economies suffer greatly and they have been unable to recover.

---

11 Kimberly Amadeo. The Balance. November 21, 2016. "US Debt by President: By Dollar and Percent."

Foreign economies experienced the same thing the US was going through. The more we weakened our currency to stimulate growth, the more foreign economies struggled as we took market share. And because we never actually recovered, foreign economies never got any downstream benefit like was anticipated.

Foreign economies tried their own QE with the same result. They didn't work for the exact same reasons. Foreign countries' government economists looked at data and believed they could create a recovery by lowering interest rates to zero and implementing QE.

But just like you and me in the US, individuals in other countries don't exist as data points that can be manipulated. These individuals were hurting just as bad if not worse. They didn't have savings, great jobs, or access to credit, either. This world-wide social experiment to generate a recovery didn't work and had the same unintended consequences.

There was one difference between the attempts at generating a recovery in foreign countries compared to the US. Those countries didn't only create bubbles in their real estate, stock markets, and collectibles. They also created a bubble in an asset that is the most important to us.

Before we move on to this special asset class we need to talk about how foreign intervention was slightly different than US intervention in attempts to stimulate their economies. And how since none of it worked, it's creating a scary situation you need to protect yourself from and also an amazing opportunity you can profit from.

Chapter 5

Bubbles Create Bubbles

Understanding the housing bubble reveals a new, more massive bubble ready to pop

The US government ended QE back in October 2014. And in December of 2015 the US raised interest rates very minimally. This was all done because economists said the economy was "recovering."

But remember what we just explained. Stock markets rose for the wrong reasons. Unemployment went down because people stopped looking for work or accepted part-time work. Auto sales went up by using the same subprime lending that took down the housing market. Corporations borrowed record amounts of money to "create" revenue growth and EPS growth.

However, the rest of the world did not stop QE or lowering interest rates. In Japan and Europe the invention of Negative Interest Rate Policy (NIRP) began. I say invention because during history there is no record of negative interest rates. In Sidney Homer's book, *A History of Interest Rates 2000 B.C. To the Present*, there's no mention of negative interest rates.

Probably we've never seen negative interest rates before because they don't make sense. They are backwards from what everyone has always understood how economics works.

If you work, earn money, and make the decision to forgo the short term pleasure of spending that money to save for a better future; you typically are paid an interest rate for making this decision.

If you need money to make a current purchase or start a business, you typically have to pay an interest rate in order for someone to give you money. You get to spend today, someone else does not. You have to pay them in order for them to forgo spending to allow you to spend.

Negative interest rates are backwards.

If you want to save money, you have to pay someone. In order to hold your money safely in a bank, you have to pay to store it there. So by not spending your money, you lose a percentage of it every year.

On the reverse, you're paid an interest rate to borrow money. So if you have no money but want to spend money today, you're paid for someone to give you money to spend.

Do you understand that? If not, I get it. It shouldn't make sense. Why on earth would someone pay you to loan you money? Why on earth would you pay someone to save your money? And if this is backwards why on earth would governments implement this policy?

Simple, government economists look at data and think everyone will behave rationally and do what data suggests. If you must pay interest to save money, clearly you'll spend it. If you get paid to borrow money, clearly you'll borrow money and spend it. NIRP is the solution to force spending and creation of economic growth.

But these economists don't understand how real people react to these policies. If you and I are forced to pay someone to save our money, we're not going to spend it. One of two things will happen. You're going to save even more money to make up for the fact you're losing money on everything you save. Or you're going to withdraw your money from the bank and stash it in your home where you don't have to pay to save.

This is exactly what happened in Japan. Sales of safes skyrocketed and stores sold out when negative interest rates were introduced. Japan had to create more large denomination bills to meet the demand. People wanted large bills so they could store more money in their homes. Spending didn't increase.

In Europe some insurance companies began looking at how much it would cost them to build a vault to store cash. They were considering whether the cost of building a vault would be cheaper than paying an interest rate to a bank to save their money.

On the other side of the spectrum, banks didn't want to lend money. They didn't want to pay people to borrow money. Banks make money by the interest rate they earn on lending it out. They can't make money by paying someone to borrow money.

Instead of having the intended results, economic growth stalled even more as nobody understood what was going on. People are so confused by negative interest rates that even less spending is occurring.

One of the only remaining options for countries to do to create economic growth in their country is to steal market share of the world economy from other countries. As we discussed earlier, this is what the US did immediately after the 2008 financial crisis. The US weakened the dollar in order to make goods and services cheaper. They believed this would create economic growth that would filter down to other countries.

But it didn't.

Now with the whole world economy struggling, countries are not willing to let another take market share. Countries are racing to weaken their currency to try and stimulate some growth in their own economy (in other worlds steal some market share).

This has led to currency wars across the world. So far most of the major countries have played nice in the currency wars, taking turns weakening. But this has not always been the case and it will not continue. It has created another big unintended consequence that we need to protect from and can profit from.

How Weak Currency Steals Market Share

As we mentioned earlier when the US weakened its currency, it stole market share because its goods and services were cheaper than foreign goods. Let's take a moment to explain this in more detail.

Every major economy is struggling right now. This is setting up a crash. Porter Stansberry of Stansberry Research stated "I'm 100% certain we're going to enter another recession next year." Stansberry continues, "What's coming in 2018 and 2019 will be the biggest economic storm of our lives. It's going to wipe out a lot of people – unemployment will go way over 10%. And more than $1 trillion worth of bonds will default. This is absolutely going to happen, because while the government can buy all the bonds it wants, it can't make them pay."[12]

China's growth is slowing. The UK and Europe economies have been slowing. Japan's economy is a mess.

When one country weakens their currency it's weakened against another currency. For instance if the US weakens against the Euro, this allows the

---

12 Porter Stansberry. Stansberry Digest. October 7th, 2016. "Porter: There is a 100% Chance of Recession Next Year."

US to produce cheaper goods and services than Europe. So the US stimulates growth while Europe suffers. Since 2009, countries have been taking turns in weakening their currencies.

Let's give an example how currency wars works. Ford is one of the top US auto manufacturers, Honda is a top Japanese manufacturer, and Volkswagen (VW) is a top European manufacturer. To simplify, we're going to assume all the parts and labor to assemble each car is done in the home country of the car company. And that they buld the exact same caliber of car and they all sell for the same price.

This isn't how it works in reality but to explain currency wars, it's best to make sure we have an apples to apples comparison.

If Japan weakens their currency, the Yen, and Europe weakens their currency, the Euro, what does this do to Ford's ability to sell cars? It would hurt their ability to sell as many cars.

Assume you are an American shopping in US dollars and you're solely shopping on price since all the cars are the same. You'll be paying US dollars no matter which car you buy. Forget for a moment that you may have a bias towards the American made car. As the economy suffers, price will become the most important factor.

VW and Honda will be able to sell their cars for fewer US dollars than Ford can. When the Yen and Euro gets weaker compared to the US dollar, it will take fewer US dollars to buy the same amount of Euros and Yen (i.e. the exchange rate goes down). Honda and VW could maintain their exact same profits in their home country currency by lowering the amount of US dollars they charge as their currency gets weaker.

The simple example above is how currency wars work. Countries are fighting over who can weaken their currency. Yes, countries want to weaken their currency so that way they can attempt to steal market share in hope of getting their economy going. The flip side is that as your currency weakens, foreign goods become more expensive. If countries import a lot— if you need imported goods to live— your cost of living goes up.

If Japan, Europe, China, and the UK all continue to struggle, these countries could be **forced** to weaken their currency. When they weaken their currency, their goods become cheaper than goods in the US. This will cause the US economy to suffer.

Now the US is set to make things worse.

The US raised interest rates once in December 2015 and once in December 2016. They are expected to raise them again. In December 2015 when they raised rates the stock market dropped. If the economy in the US is declining and the stock market dropped the last time the US raised interest rates, why would they raise rates again?

Warning: Everything from this point forward is going to sound completely contradictory and backwards. It's going to sound confusing. Truthfully, it's hard to understand every time I explain it to someone or write it. But please read it carefully and with an open mind that, indeed, it should sound that way. That's how bad this situation is getting, how the government is running out of tools, and why you need to protect yourself and take advantage of the profit opportunities.

Back in the first couple of chapters we mentioned that lowering interest rates is one of the government economists' best tools to stop or fight off recessions. When recessions hit, the government economists want to lower interest rates to stimulate the economy. This is because they believe when you lower interest rates, it encourages borrowing and subsequent spending. It also discourages saving and hence spending. But remember, this doesn't work because that's not how reality works for you and me.

Now, the US government economists are trying to figure out how to raise interest rates because they also believe a recession is coming. They are trying to get interest rates up for the only purpose of being able to lower them as soon as the recession hits. Higher interest rates mean a strong US dollar which will surely bring the recession about quicker. But government economists don't care because they believe they need the tool of lowering interest rates in order to stop the inevitable recession!

Mainstream news outlets and financial media have been saying the US should have raised interest rates a long time ago. They should have raised them more often and quicker. That the economy could have handled them a while ago but now it may not. I don't know whether any of that is true or not. All I know is that right now we are on the verge of a recession.

Higher interest rates will make the US dollar stronger which will cause foreign goods and services to become cheaper. The US economy will suffer even more as corporate and private debts become too costly to pay back. When they default, it will trigger a recession. And the government is only raising interest rates so they can turn around and lower them once the recession hits. Here's the thing, even if they do raise them they're still at historical lows. They will not have much room to lower interest rates without taking them negative because they will still be really low.

When the US economy enters a recession, we have no room to lower interest rates since they're at historical lows. As other countries continue to weaken their currency to try to stimulate growth in their own economies, will the US go to **negative interest rates**? I don't know but it wouldn't shock me. We've never seen negative interest rates over the course of history because they don't make sense. But the world has them so why couldn't they come to the US?

The other tool the US government will most likely try again is more QE. Remember the US stopped QE back in October 2014. Once the recession hits it may have to try it again. But in the past, it didn't have the intended consequences. It added to the government debt, corporate debt, student loan debt, and auto debt. It caused the bond market and stock market to rise substantially. But it didn't get the economy going or create any inflation.

If we add more debt, it's going to have even less impact than it had before. We're reaching the law of diminishing returns with debt (I actually think it's already been reached). This basically says as you use more and more of a tool, the returns diminish and eventually become nothing or worse. We had very little impact the first time we did QE and ZIRP. With debt at historical highs, I see the impact of QE and ZIRP (or even NIRP) being basically nothing. Or worse!

Remember during the housing crisis, greed caused everyone to believe home prices would always go up. And in recent memory that is all that had ever happened to home prices. Buyers were getting higher loans than they could afford to repay and overpaying for high priced homes. But what happened?

They ran out of buyers. The 1% stops investing. The speculative flippers stop getting financing. People stop buying... and start defaulting. Market glut. Housing tanks.

If a recession comes and the government tries QE, ZIRP, or NIRP as its regular tools because they "always" work during a recession; if debt is at all-time highs, who is going to lend more money? If you already have a substantial amount of debt who is going to borrow more money?

The wealthy 1% are already calling for a top in the bond market and speculating that the stock market is overvalued. If the 1% are saying there is no money to make, that is the first sign that people are pulling out.

From the *Stansberry Digest*:

"David Tepper – the billionaire founder of hedge fund Appaloosa Management – admitted that he is 'pretty cautious' on the market today...'I just don't see the market having the ability to move up that much." More from the Digest, "Billionaire Carl Icahn said he, too, is cautious...He believes we have a 'false market' – largely propped up by central-bank manipulation – and said that many S&P 500 companies are 'way overvalued' today. Former hedge-fund manager and Goldman Sachs alum Raoul Pal shared a warning…that the U.S. will fall into recession within a year: 'The business cycle points to that… and 100% of all two-term elections have had recessions within 12 months since 1910."[13]

Just like they were the first sign of buyers pulling out of the housing market, they're the first sign of buyers of debt and stocks coming out of the market. This is going to cause QE and ZIRP to have less and less impact, almost no impact. When the economy doesn't recover even with additional debt, no interest rates, and increased money supply, the people who borrowed more than they could afford for auto loans will begin to default. Corporations that took on more debt than they should have to buy back shares or buy revenue growth with low interest rates will default.

As these defaults grow, it will spread through the overall economy that is already in a recession. And eventually it will lead to a stock market crash.

Yes, I believe there is a bubble in the bond market and that the bond market is going to crash. But that is not the bubble you need to protect yourself from or profit off. Most likely you are not exposed to high-yield bonds or low end investment grade debt. And profiting off the bond crash is a more complicated strategy. If you're interested there are some great services that focus on these exact trends and I will feature them in Appendix 3 on reviews and recommendations of newsletters.

The bubble I'm referring to is the US dollar bubble. The US dollar is in trouble and the trouble has already begun. But you will not hear about this in mainstream media or financial outlets. You'll actually hear the exact opposite which is why it's so important you pay attention to this.

---

13 Justin Brill. Stansberry Digest. October 18th 2016. "New Warnings from the World's Greatest Investors."

Remember the US economy is on the verge of an imminent recession. But the US government is also going to raise interest rates which will strengthen the US dollar. This is while other major economies like Europe and Japan have negative interest rates.

In the real world, the US dollar should get stronger due to the underlying US economy. But the US economy has been declining for 5 consecutive quarters as of Q2 2016 and is about to enter a recession. This should cause the US dollar to be weakening. But it's not for several reasons.

One is because the US government economists are going to raise interest rates for the sole purpose of giving them a little room to lower them when the recession comes. Another is other countries already have lower interest rates and even negative interest rates. This makes the dollar stronger than their currency.

If you were in Japan and could put your money in Yen which you have to pay to save, or you could put it in US dollars which earn a tiny return, which would you do? And if the US raises interest rates even more money will come into US dollars.

In the discussion around inflation, we mentioned demand for US dollars should come because the US economy is booming and there is foreign demand for US goods and services. We're going to have increased demand for US dollars despite a declining US economy **only because the US dollar is stronger than every other foreign currency.**

Remember I believe inflation already exists; it just doesn't exist in consumer goods. Since 2009, we've greatly increased the money supply and all levels of debt. This didn't grow the economy or create consumer price inflation. It created an extremely over-valued stock market, bond market, high-end real estate market, and collectibles market. This increased money supply and debt allowed the 1% to create asset bubbles. If these bubbles pop, that inflation that should exist will show up.

On top of the inflation we should already have, we're heading towards a recession where we'll get more money supply and government debt. And maybe even negative interest rates.

So don't be fooled by the US dollar's strength. It's just the best option in a declining world economy that is strangled by record debt levels.

It's backwards and it's going to end badly. Understanding all this will help you protect yourself and profit in the future. Now you know how to interpret the mainstream media and financial outlets. And you see why you need to act differently than the 99% if you want better results.

Now, our second break…. Prospering is the best revenge

INTERLUDE 2: Don't Get Mad, Protect and Profit

After everything I just explained, you may feel mad, upset, deceived, or frustrated. And with what's coming in the next section these emotions may come even more to the forefront. You could also be scared.

I understand this. I used to feel the same way. The government is basically creating this environment that allows these bubbles and bursts to occur. And it doesn't punish anyone responsible for causing them. The 1% profit greatly while we struggle to get ahead. It's complicated and confusing and sounds like you need to be a rocket scientist to know how to protect yourself and profit from the opportunities.

Please drop these emotions now. Don't be scared. When you have knowledge you can understand and implement. Don't feel mad or deceived. Now you have the power to take control and profit.

That's what I did. I stopped getting angry at everyone creating bubbles and causing these crises. I stopped being upset at the government for creating the environment that allows it and for thinking about everything in terms of academia and data you can manipulate instead of real people.

Emotions fog your brain and prevent you from taking clear action. They can incapacitate you and cause you to make poor choices. Let them go.

Once I let these emotions go, clarity came to me. I realized I enjoy reading and learning about this stuff. I read independent financial newsletters that I pay for every single day. When most people are watching TV, drinking with friends, going out on dates, playing with their kids; I'm reading financial newsletters to understand how this all works.

I realized that my skills as an accountant gives me the ability to connect the ideas together and explain them simply so people who have different priorities or who don't enjoy or understand this, can still protect and profit themselves.

So please let these emotions go before we continue.

Understand that nobody cares about your finances as much as you do. And everyone cares about their own finances more than yours. It's natural. Human nature is to take care of yourself and your family first. This may be at the expense of you because for someone to make money, someone is probably losing money in today's world.

By no means am I condoning the behavior of crooks. And by no means am I suggesting I'm the only person operating in your best interest. My writing this book is just as selfish as everyone else. I enjoy this stuff. I enjoy learning. By teaching others, I learn more myself. I hope to use income from this book to invest in more financial newsletters.

I'm also writing this because I want the world to be a better place. The more we ALL profit the better it becomes. If you're able to protect your family, profit off opportunities to get ahead, and spend your time doing what you love without financial worries, you'll be happier and the world will be a happier place. This will make my life better than any amount of money.

So remove any negative or scared emotions and read the rest of this book without allowing them to come in. Just realize you will hear something different from mainstream media and financial outlets than what is actually happening. Take care not to be sucked in by their fanning the emotions of fear or greed as these bubbles grow and burst.

You'll soon learn that it's very simple to protect yourself. And it's very simple to profit. You don't need a degree in finance. You don't need to read financial news and reports all day long. You can prosper knowing what I've told you and just a little more about finances. I'll tell you exactly what you can do without giving specific recommendations. And if you want specific recommendations, I'll refer you to the absolute best research available for these recommendations.

On your side, you need discipline to save money and the ability to take action. You need to take control of your finances. You can understand it's a good thing to think differently from everyone you come into contact with.

You can protect your and your family's finances. And you can break from the crowd and get ahead financially. Simply and easily!

Chapter 6

Planning for the Unpredictable

We don't know what's next, what will cause it, when it will crash; and the exact opposite will happen before it occurs. But here are possible scenarios

At the end of Chapter 5, we touched on how the new debt bubble, caused by government debt, is the US dollar. And it looks very similar to how the housing bubble was fueled by credit. The housing bubble burst when there were no more buyers, less credit, defaults, foreclosed homes, increasing supply and reducing demand.

The time will come when we'll see buyers of US dollars dry up. This will cause a pop in the US dollar bubble, inflation like never seen before, and a financial crisis of magnitudes greater than back in 2008. The US housing bubble was bad, but was one sector of the economy. The US dollar is the main currency used around the World!

In this chapter I'll show you several things that could cause this to happen. These are things you may not know are even occurring since there is little coverage in mainstream and financial news outlets. And you may even hear contradictory things as well.

Before continuing, let's set expectations. I don't know that any one of the things I'll discuss will happen. I don't know exactly how any of them could play out. And I certainly don't know when any of them would begin to happen. I can't predict the future. If I could, I'd already be a billionaire. But I'm not. I'm just a normal, hard-working American like you, who wants to protect what I've earned and learn how to get ahead.

All I can do is describe what's occurring around the world. And I can share what happened when these conditions occurred in the past.

I'm going to speculate on how things will play out, and what you'll hear in the mainstream news and from your financial advisor before the crisis hits. Not because I truly believe I'll be 100% correct but because I want you to be prepared for what's going on. And when you hear contradictory information from mainstream media, you know why you should not trust it completely.

I'm confident the over-arching thesis of the US dollar bubble bursting will occur. And I believe it will happen over the next 5-10 years. But I also know government economists get very creative trying to protect their own interests which can make the situation worse while pushing it down the road.

What's written below is a speculation about what could occur to lead towards the dollar bubble bursting, creating our opportunity to profit. Any one of these could or could not happen and any one alone could cause the crisis to begin. They may or may not come in this order.

Here are the risks facing your investments in the coming year or five.

1. Bond Crisis – as early as 2017.

Triggers to watch for:

1. **Corporate debt is at an all-time high.** It's percentage of GDP is around 45% which is typically the high it reaches before the bond market crashes. Government debt is at an all-time high and almost $8 trillion was added since the last financial crisis to try to generate a recovery that never really happened.

2. **Billionaires (the 1%) are beginning to say they see a bubble in bonds.** They are no longer investing in bonds which is the first sign the market is reaching its top, just like it was in housing. The US economy is about to enter a recession and the US is going to raise interest rates.

3. **The government steps in with more QE** and lowering of interest rates back to zero or negative. But we have too much debt for that to work. Negative interest rates are backwards and people don't respond in real life the way government economists believe they should according to data.

4. **Large quantities of debt come due.** In the housing bubble, one of the triggers was variable interest rate loans coming due and owners not being able to refinance because their home price stopped rising. In 2017, large quantities of corporate debt will begin coming due and need refinancing. As companies' earnings continue to deteriorate and we enter a recession, they will be unable to refinance at the same low rates... or at all. Companies will begin to have their ratings lowered by ratings agencies.

All of this will lead to defaults. Contagion will spread throughout the ever connected world economy. Contagion is when one incident spreads through many different aspects of the economy and affects more than just the company initially in trouble.

As one company defaults on their loans, it affects the one who holds that loan. Whoever holds that loan (most likely a financial institution or corporate investor) will now have fewer assets as they write off the loan. That company will now be in much worse financial shape. This could cause the financial company or corporate investor to have its rating dropped.

If a company's rating drops, it may now fall out of investment grade. Pension funds and certain mutual and hedge funds, according to their rules, cannot own bonds below investment grade. They'll be forced to sell. Demand goes down and supply goes up. Stock prices drop.

Owners of that company will see their assets drop in value. This could cause institutional owners to default on their loans or have their rating lowered.

If any of these assets were purchased on margin (borrowed money, like was key in the housing crash and financial crisis), companies may be required to sell other assets (stocks and bonds) in order to raise cash to pay back their margin. You're given margin based upon the amount of assets you have. If your assets drop due to a bond defaulting or stock of a company whose bond defaulted dropping, you have to pay back some of your margin loan. This could require more selling.

All of this connectedness could lead to a complete collapse of the high-yield and low-end investment grade bond market. The low-end investment grade bond market is at risk because it loaned money to companies that normally only qualify for high-yield loans. In other words, it sounds very familiar to banks giving mortgages to people with bad credit and for more than they can afford.

Porter Stansberry is predicting a complete collapse in the bond market in his daily *Stansberry Digest*. "Next year is going to be ugly for stocks. But it will be even worse for corporate bonds. In 2017, we'll see the first maturities on the huge amount of junk bonds that were issued in the record issuance cycle between 2010 and 2015. Roughly $125 billion will be due. The default rate across the sector will approach 10%. It will be much more difficult, and maybe impossible, for companies to refinance these obligations...If we're in a recession next year...look out. All of these debts will be seen as un-financeable...The fact is, most of these loans should have never been made. These companies are vastly overleveraged. And their financial condition, as a group, hasn't improved since 2010...It has gotten worse...A reckoning is coming."[14]

After it was determined our next President would be Donald J. Trump, Stansberry said why he won't be able to save us.

"The Republicans believe tax cuts and military spending are the basic formula for economic prosperity. The people cheering today believe that Trump's wall (his announced infrastructure spending), his tax cuts, and his estimated $6 trillion budget deficit over four years will create winners in the stock market and wealth for our nation. In some limited ways, that will prove to be true.

"But in other, far more important ways, the idea that government spending and government debt is a positive force in the economy [is] fatally wrong... It's hard to believe that the president can do anything to alter the course of our ongoing credit-default cycle. The only prediction that's consistent with sound economy theory is that the government is going to make this default cycle a lot worse."[15]

Stansberry has even launched a newsletter designed to profit off the coming default cycle and a newsletter on how to invest in the quality bonds that drop in price with the bad bonds. When the markets collapse, not only the bad

---

14 Porter Stansberry. Stansberry Digest. October 7th, 2016. "Porter: There is a 100% Chance of Recession Next Year."

15 Porter Stansberry. Stansberry Digest. November 9th, 2016. "Why Trump's Plans Won't Save Us."

stocks drop. Good stocks do too, and this creates buying opportunities. You can learn more about these newsletters in Appendix 3.

We're already on the brink of recession. Earnings have been dropping. If the bond market crashes, the stock market could follow.

2. Possible Bank Crisis

European banks are on the verge of collapse.

The world's oldest and third-largest bank in Italy could fail at any moment. Banca Monte dei Paschi di Sienna (BMP) failed the European Central Banks's (ECB) recent stress test and is required to raise capital. BMP has the highest ratio of non-performing loans (NPLs) of any Italian Bank.[16]

The largest bank in Germany, Deutsche Bank, is on the verge of crisis. From the *Stansberry Digest*, "Deutsche has roughly $2 trillion in assets. That's almost 11% of U.S. GDP…the bank can sustain losses of only 2.9% before its equity capital is wiped out…According to the International Monetary Fund, Deutsche is the riskiest financial institution in the world… the 'most important net contributor to [global] systemic risks." The *Digest* continues, "We could soon see the equivalent of a 2008 crisis in Europe. Rest assured financial problems coming to roost abroad will spark a global selloff in equities."[17]

To make matters worse Jim Rickards, editor of *Intelligence Triggers*, says,

---

16 Jim Rickards. Intelligence Triggers. September 20, 2016. "New Kissinger Cross: This Crisis Indicator Just Flashed Red" and Nick Giambruno. Crisis Investing. August 2016, Issue 3.8. "Countdown to a Stock Market Collapse of Historical Proportions."

17 Porter Stansberry. Stansberry Digest. September 30th, 2016. "How to Make a Fortune as $300 Billion in Corporate Debt Explodes."

"...the U.S. Department of Justice announced that it was seeking $14 billion to settle charges that Deutsche Bank engaged in misleading sales practices with regard to residential mortgage backed securities between 2005 and 2007. Of course, that's just a claim. But, even if Deutsche Bank settles the case for a fraction of that amount, say $5 billion, it will significantly impair an already weak capital base."[18]

And remember, everything is connected. Banks operate worldwide. If these banks fail, it will spread through contagion to US financial institutions.

This could trigger the bond collapse. The bond collapse could trigger these banks failing and the Euro failing.

3. Stock Market Collapse

The stock market is also in bubble territory. Any of these items above could set off a stock market crash.

But, and this will sound contradictory, I think the stock market will go higher first. Why? Because mainstream media and financial outlets are still fearful of the market. The market does not typically crash when mainstream is fearful. It collapses when all fear is gone. This is what happened in the housing crash.

Personally, I don't think any of the above will happen until the stock market climbs higher to more all-time highs and everyone becomes bullish (except for the 1%). This has already begun now that the uncertainty of the US presidential election is over.

Our 2016 US presidential election was extremely negative and nothing about policy. This created fear in the markets. That's over. We now know Donald J. Trump will be our next President and the stock market has shot higher.

---

18 Jim Rickards. Intelligence Triggers. September 20, 2016. "New Kissinger Cross: This Crisis Indicator Just Flashed Red"

On the night of election, the Dow plunged and gold futures rose higher. But by morning this was completely reversed and the Dow was up and gold was down by Wednesday market close. This is what happened to markets when "Brexit" (the UK leaving the EU) won. The market went down and gold went up. But after a short period it returned to new highs.

Personally, I thought the market would have stayed lower and gold higher for a few days. This thought process came from watching what happened with "Brexit." But it didn't even take one day for the market to begin marching higher as certainty was restored.

Even though a recession is inevitable, earnings are dropping, and the market should go down; the new president-elect has had an influence on the market. Even if you don't like who won, the market has calmed down and is pricing in its expectations of what will happen under the new President.

The market will expect easy money (low interest rates and QE) to continue because it will have to in order to stop the recession. And President Trump is declaring lower taxes. Investors are hoping Donald Trump will be another President Reagan who gives us a booming economy by lowering taxes, spending on the military, and rebuilding America.

Defense stocks, industrial stocks (those involved in infrastructure rebuilding), and the general market are soaring because of this.

With lower taxes, earnings of companies will rise even if the economy or company does not improve. Republicans say the lower taxes will allow reinvestment into the business and create more jobs. In theory, this makes sense. But corporate debt is at all-time highs. **The savings from lower taxes will go towards reducing debt not into creating jobs and growing the economy. These unintended consequences will stall any economic boom.**

The infrastructure spending and military rebuilding will create more revenues for companies involved in these industries. Their earnings will increase. Republicans are saying this will create more jobs, further stimulating the economy. In theory this makes sense as well. But student loan debt, auto debt, and government debt are at all-time highs. Once people finally get back to work, they'll be paying off debt or saving the money to prepare against losing their job again. People have been out of work for so long, they won't trust it will last. This spending will not have a trickle-down effect throughout the entire economy. It will stop one-level removed.

And because government debt is already at all-time highs, creating more debt for this spending will continue to have less and less impact. Unintended consequences.

Despite the economy not being stimulated by all this spending and lower taxes, earnings will go up. No President wants to begin in a recession and will rely on the same government economist's tools in an attempt to avoid it. This will allow the market to rise higher, and more and more people will begin buying even though the market is already over-valued and at all-time highs.

Yes that's right, I believe the market will go higher exactly when it should go lower. Here are four reasons why stocks might go much higher before they drop.

* People see stocks and bonds as the only place if they want to earn income
* People lose sight of logic, reality, and risks when blinded by greed
* Mainstream media and financial outlets claim all is well, keep investing
* Foreign investment in the US Stock market

Japan tried all sorts of methods to stimulate their economy and none of it has worked. They are buying Japanese corporate bonds with government debt. They are buying Japanese stocks with government debt. A *Bloomberg* headline in Oct 2016 read: "Owning Half of Japan's ETF Market Might Not Be Enough for Kuroda." Its first sentence read: "Japan's central bank already owns more than half of the nation's market for exchange-traded stock funds, and that might just be the start."[19]

Haruhiko Karudo is the head of Japan's central bank. Also, from *True Wealth*, "Mr. K said the Japanese government will 'steadily implement its large scale stimulus measures, amounting to 28 trillion yen.' That's around US$250 billion in stimulus."[20]

Next the Japanese government may begin buying US stocks. Yes, the stock market may rise because the Japanese government is creating money through debt and buying the stock market.

Switzerland already has $62B of government reserves invested in the US market and is expected to increase their ownership.[21]

Once Japan realizes their newest plan doesn't work they will seriously consider buying US stocks—especially now that the fear of the presidential election is over and the market has started marching higher. Japan will get caught up in the greed of seeing huge profits in a rising US market just like mainstream media and the 99%.

When individuals, corporations, hedge funds, and governments are all investing in stocks, isn't this a sign that we are about out of buyers? When there are no new buyers a top is near, and then, a sudden slip down the slope to a crash.

---

19 Steve Sjuggerud. True Wealth. December 2016. "Little-Known 'Mr. K' Just Set Up the Best Trade of Our Lives."
20 Steve Sjuggerud. True Wealth. December 2016. "Little-Known 'Mr. K' Just Set Up the Best Trade of Our Lives."
21 Reuters. August 30, 2016. "Swiss Central bank steps up stock buying spree."

So when you hear mainstream media and financial outlets touting, "you have to be in this market, it just keeps going higher." Be fearful, not greedy. Understand why it's going higher and that it could crash any moment. There are simple ways to safeguard when you have this knowledge. You'll be protected and prepared to profit.

Again this doesn't mean you sell any quality dividend paying or value stocks you plan to own for the long term. I own these types of stocks and am not selling, nor will I sell, when the market crashes. In fact, I'm still looking to buy small positions in the few undervalued stocks that do exist, to hold for the long term. But get out of any risky, speculative, no earnings type of stocks at this time.

4. Watch Out For Inflation

The world governments and companies could benefit from inflation. They've tried to create it with QE, ZIRP, and NIRP, but have failed. Inflation favors the borrower, but does not favor the saver. So why does the world need inflation?

It's the only way to pay back all the government debt. This is not a political statement this is reality. Governments spend too much money on entitlements, wars, clean energy, and pretty much everything they are involved in. Once government begins spending money, it is nearly impossible to cut it. Politicians will not cut spending because it will cause them to not be re-elected.

And raising taxes won't get the US out of debt because we have too many costly entitlements. And President Trump says he will lower taxes. Even if you wanted to raise taxes to pay off government debt, it doesn't work. You can believe this or not, but if you look at history, regardless of the individual and corporate tax rate, individual and corporate tax receipts as a percentage of GDP remain very flat.

If you cannot cut spending and cannot increase tax revenues as a percentage of GDP no matter how high you raise tax rates for individuals and corporations, how do you pay back your debt? With inflation.

Remember, inflation makes your money buy less of what it could in the past so for an individual inflation is bad. If your income is not going up as fast as inflation, you will be able to buy less goods and services than you can today for the same amount of money.

But for debt, it works the other way around. If the government has inflation, they can use these inflated and weakened dollars to pay back debt that was borrowed under more valuable and stronger dollars.

Inflation is essentially a tax on you and me. We're unable to purchase as many goods and services but the government can pay back debt without cutting spending or raising actual tax revenues. This is why the government needs inflation. This is why they are trying everything they can do to create inflation.

But if and when they get inflation, it's unlikely they will be able to control it.

As world economies continue to struggle, there is another "government type entity" that will try to get inflation: The International Monetary Fund (IMF).

5. The International Monetary Fund

The IMF is essentially a government bank for the world governments. They even have their own money called special drawing rights (SDRs). You've probably never heard of this before because you cannot own them. They are only issued to governments. Basically they are a weighted basket of major currencies that governments can use to spend on large governmental projects.

Well something very interesting just happened with these SDRs. They used to only be valued based on four countries' currencies. The US Dollar, Japanese Yen, British Pound, and European Euro. However, very recently they added in the Chinese Renminbi. Not only did they just include it in the basket of currencies, they gave it the third highest weighting behind the US dollar and Euro.

Why did they do this? Jim Rickards, former advisor for the CIA and author of many books such as the *The Death of Money, Currency Wars* and several great financial newsletters (see appendix 3), believes it's because the IMF is going to try to create inflation once governments fail to do so during the next recession.

> "SDRs are not used for ordinary stimulus in recessions. SDRs are used to deal with liquidity crises. They are also used when crises of confidence in the international monetary system occur. SDRs are like a secret weapon that global elites deploy as needed to prop up the global financial system."[22]

Since China is the second largest economy and a large holder of US dollar reserves, they needed to get China's currency in the basket before this time comes. Rickards says:

> "SDRs are useful only if they can be swapped for other reserve currencies to prop up banks and liquidate panicked sellers of stocks.... When your neighbors are in full panic mode, they won't want SDRs from Citibank; they'll want dollars. But who will swap dollars for the SDRs printed by the IMF? The answer is China...But there's a catch. China will engage in SDR/dollar swaps only if the yuan [Chinese Renminbi] is included in the SDR....

---

22 Jim Rickards. Strategic Intelligence. 7/29/2016. "The only way to own new world money."

"The rush to include China in the SDR should be seen as global monetary elites getting their ducks in a row before the next panic comes to destroy your portfolio....The U.S. Dollar will be reduced to the status of a local currency. In other words, the dollar will still be used for local transactions in the U.S., but it will no longer be the benchmark for sound reserve management. The impact on the dollar from the issuance of SDRs will be highly inflationary."[23]

Rickards believes that when the next recession hits and all the government institutions fail to create inflation, that the IMF will issue massive amounts of SDR's. These will be issued to government entities for spending on world projects, such as clean energy, infrastructure and the like.

The intention will be the same as what each individual government tried. Infuse money into the economy to create more spending and hence inflation.

But the outcome will be the same. Yes, spending may occur on all these projects and it may temporarily create some jobs. But since we'll already be in a recession, the jobs will just be restoring some of what was lost. And just like what is happening today, with low interest rates, a bad economy, and uncertainty with what is going on; people won't spend the money.

Whoever earns that money will just save it. And since these will be government projects, the amount of money being issued will not have a 1 for 1 benefit due to natural government inefficiencies.

Once this doesn't work, there will only be one option left. This is the basis of this book and your key to protect your assets and profit from events.

---

23 Jim Rickards. Strategic Intelligence. 7/29/2016. "The only way to own new world money."

6. The US Political Turmoil and Gridlock

Unless you've been living under a rock, you know how crazy the US presidential election season was. The democrats almost elected a socialist and instead elected the most corrupt candidate in history. The republicans elected someone with egotistical dictator tendencies. Both of the actual nominees had the highest disapproval rating ever.

Honestly, I'm not shocked Trump was elected. In my opinion all politicians are corrupt and the two parties just approach corruption in different ways. Neither really tries to help America. They're only pandering to the 50% that support their side of corruption.

After 8 years of a Democratic president, the liberal side is used to the Democratic nonsense and just hears more of the same coming from the Democratic nominee. But the conservatives are sick and tired of 8 years of Democrats and so turned out in numbers to elect a Republican. This is no different than how 8 years of Republican President Bush, left conservatives desensitized to the Republican nonsense. Then, liberals were sick and tired of 8 years of Republicans so they got out and voted in President Obama.

We swing from one side of the pendulum to the other side. Never stopping in the middle to do what will actually help the US economy and Americans. This is why the election cycle is getting more and more violent. This is why we now have riots opposing the elected President. This is why people are scared to even say who they support.

And leaving problems unfixed just creates more and more debt, a weaker dollar, and anger from one side to the other.

7. The Oil Danger

Up until 1971 the US dollar had been pegged to a percentage of gold. In 1971 this peg was removed. This move alone should have created inflation as the money supply of dollars increased to exceed the US economic growth. However, at the same time something else occurred that most people don't know.

The US was concerned about the availability of oil and the Middle East's, particularly Saudi Arabia's, ability to manipulate oil prices which could hurt the US economy. Robert W. Tucker, an academic, wrote an article that appeared in *Commentary Magazine* in 1975 titled "Oil: The Issue of American Intervention." It described how military intervention could be used to take control of the Saudi Oil. This was political posturing but it made Saudi Arabia willing to make a deal with the US.

Jim Rickards wrote in *Strategic Intelligence*:

"The Saudis would agree to price oil in dollars, and to reinvest those dollars in U.S. Treasury securities and Eurodollar deposits in U.S. Banks. In exchange, the U.S. would take steps to stabilize the exchange value of the dollar, and would agree to sell advanced weapons to the Kingdom.... Once oil was priced in dollars, every country in the world would need dollars because every country in the world needed oil."[24]

What this means it that it created almost unlimited demand for US dollars.

Every country needed US dollars, not because our economy was great and they wanted to purchase US goods and services, which is a valid reason to demand dollars. But rather because they **had** to convert their currency to US dollars in order to buy oil. And everyone was buying oil from the Saudis.

When the US removed the dollar from the gold peg and we continued to "print" money to increase our economy, we should have had massive inflation.

---

24 Jim Rickards. Strategic Intelligence. August 2016. "R.I.P. Petrodollar: March 1975-Sept. 4, 2016."

But we didn't because we basically had our currency backed by oil. That was the Saudi Arabia oil. But that could quickly change.

The US now has enough oil and natural gas to become self-sufficient. We no longer need the Saudi oil. This is partly what led to the crash in oil prices. As we explained earlier with commodity cycles when the price of oil was high it led to significant investment. This led to the US figuring out how to find and extract more oil within the USA— more than we could ever need. Supply exceeded demand as the economy headed for recession and the price of oil crashed.

With the US needing less and less of the Saudi's oil, we have started distancing ourselves from being their partner. The Saudi's are believed to be responsible for providing financing to the terrorist attackers from 9/11. Rickards says:

> "Relations between Saudi Arabia and the U.S. have deteriorated sharply over the course of the Obama administration. The primary cause was the Iran-U.S. Nuclear negotiations and what amounts to the U.S. recognizing Iran as the leading regional power....The U.S. also released a formerly top secret 28-page section of the 9/11 Commission Report that clearly reveals links between members of the Saudi royal family and the 9/11 hijackers and Al Qaeda....The conversion of oil prices away from dollars to some alternative is just a matter of time."[25]

Exchanges are being created that allow oil to be traded in currencies other than the US dollar. This will drastically reduce demand for US dollars and could trigger a pop in the bubble.

On top of that, oil outside the US is priced according to "Brent." This is an average of the price of oil coming out of the British sector of the North Sea, which hardly produces any oil anymore. The Russians are working to

---

25 Jim Rickards. Strategic Intelligence. August 2016. "R.I.P. Petrodollar: March 1975-Sept. 4, 2016."

get rid of the Brent pricing and create their own new pricing for the European benchmark since they produce substantially more oil. This again would reduce demand for US dollars and could pop the bubble.

8. International Conflicts

In the Middle East, Russia is challenging the US military might. They are becoming more aggressive and seeing how we respond. I don't believe the Russians want to start a war with the US but they want to show that the United States is not interested in stopping their aggression. Look, I don't want us to get into a war. I'm just saying if the US begins to appear weak militarily, this could cause a pop in the dollar bubble.

In the South China Sea, there are disputes about who controls certain areas. China built islands by moving sand to these areas and is setting up military operations. They want to control fishing and push Japan out of what had been international waters. The US has allowed this and not intervened. China is showing their military might and the US weakness.

Again, I'm for us not getting involved but this could cause a pop in the dollar bubble.

China also recently got their currency added to the IMF. Their stock exchange is going to be added into the MSCI emerging markets index at a substantial weighting. Their currency is becoming more trusted and China is feverishly building their gold reserves to put their reserve percentage of gold on par with Western countries. China is trying to establish itself as the new power. This could cause a pop in the US dollar bubble.

9. Governmental Overreach

In Cyprus, when the country's banks defaulted a few years ago, banks shuttered for a few days. Deposit accounts were "taxed" by taking away money from the wealthiest individuals in order to recapitalize the banks. This was not voted on by the public; it was ruled on and decided on by government.

In Greece, when the country's banks defaulted a few years ago, banks shuttered for a few days. There was no physical cash available. People waited in line at ATM's for hours and the ATM's ran out of cash.

When we see these things happening in other civilized democracies, we have to be aware of the risks to us and our money. I hope none of this happens in the US. I hope things continue to go well. But as a realist, I see a number of warning signs that would cause a crash and wipe out many people's assets. To recap:

* Our recent presidential election cycle which was the craziest in history and historic congressional gridlock preventing important reforms
* Negative interest rates and the danger of falling bond prices
* Fed raising rates just to lower them when the recession comes
* The failure of QE and zero interest rates
* The risks of inflation or deflation triggering a collapse in governments' and companies' ability to pay off their debts
* Our unsupportable level of debt at home and world wide
* International conflicts threatening more military spending
* Oil and commodity cycles
* The International Monetary Fund and the change in the prominence of the US dollar
* Government overreach and instant "taxes" on our savings
* Undercapitalized banks collapsing
* Stock and bond market volatility and instability

To close this chapter, beware. When you see the stock market rising and everyone jumping in, it doesn't mean it's rising for good reason. It could be that bubble about to burst.

When you see the US dollar rising and getting stronger, everyone saying it's the only safe currency, beware! It doesn't mean it's rising because our economy is doing well and for good reason. It could be because it's the best economy in a shrinking world economy, paying zero interest rates when everyone else is negative, and for the exact opposite reason it should. This means it's about to crash. Beware!

We have never been in this situation before so we can't look back in history for guidance on what might happen. The world economy has never been like this so it's impossible to predict how it will actually end. But one thing is true. All paper currencies over the history of humans have always failed. We think the US dollar will never fail but it has only really been around in its current form since 1971.

The last chapter gives you options to prepare you for what could happen and how it could play out.

The US dollar bubble is going to get bigger and then pop. It could happen next year. It could happen 5 years from now. But it's going to happen and I believe within the next 3-7 years. And I would lean on the shorter side.

Luckily there's a low cost way to protect yourself. And luckily, this same method is also a low risk way to profit substantially. This is also a form of financial insurance. But you have to be willing to do what's uncomfortable because it's not what everyone around you will do. And it's not what everyone on mainstream media and financial outlets will tell you to do.

But remember, the 99% are who get hurt during crisis. You need to do what the 1% are willing to do. You can. And it's simple and easy.

Chapter 7

● ● ●

How to Protect Yourself and PROSPER to FINANCIAL FREEDOM

Protecting your investments and taking care of your needs now and your future prosperity takes a multi-step approach. First, we need to deal with where you are right now, financially. And we need to protect you from possible immediate dangers. Then, we need to set you up to potentially prosper and gain substantial wealth by investing strategically based on what you now know.

This is an eight step process. You may find you've already done some of the steps. If so, congratulations! My recommendation is that you follow the steps in order to gain the best chance of a wealthy future.

#1 Method to PROTECT Yourself during the Coming Financial Crisis: Cash

Save 2-3 months' worth of physical cash in your home. Even though I believe the dollar is going to collapse, when it does or right before it does, there could be a shortage in cash. Remember in Greece, ATM's ran out of cash. In Cyprus banks shuttered and taxed your cash.

If there is ever a dollar shortage, you will not be able to get money out of the bank. And if banks are closing and we have a credit crisis, you will not be able to use credit cards. If this were to happen it should end quickly.

But, for peace of mind, save 2-3 months' worth of cash in your home. And I mean for everything. Your mortgage, car payment, gas, food, whatever you spend money or credit on each month.

This is a crisis hedge and hopefully will never be needed. But if the time comes, you won't be able to get it from your bank and will be glad you did this. This cash may ultimately become worth much less if the US dollar collapses but before then you may need it to survive. It's worth the risk of the money becoming worth nothing to know you'll still be able to eat and get around if there becomes a cash shortage.

#2 Method to PROTECT Yourself during the Coming Financial Crisis: Gold

This opportunity has the greatest potential to preserve and prosper your assets, in my opinion. This is a huge, once in a lifetime opportunity to think outside of the 99% and mainstream financial outlets to set yourself up to break ahead.

Let me tell you why I believe gold could go much, much higher— even to $5k-$10k per ounce over the next 3-7 years.

Back in Chapter 6, I mentioned that if individual country governments fail to create inflation (which they have) and the IMF tries and fails, there would be one option left to surely create inflation.

This came from Jim Rickards. He said the US government could immediately raise the price of gold. They would do this by saying they'll buy gold at $4,995 per ounce and sell it at $5,005 per ounce. This would immediately raise the price of gold to $5,000.

If gold were raised to $5k per ounce overnight, this would immediately create massive inflation. Rickards also said that if this is not enough inflation for as bad as things get, they could easily just raise the price again— this time to $10k per ounce by becoming a buyer at $9,995 per ounce and seller at $10,005 per ounce. But don't think for a moment that you can wait until the first time they raise the price of gold to buy. You won't be able to. There most likely will be no gold available. The purchasing power of the US dollar would dive. However, if you already have gold in your portfolio then you'd be protected.

Porter Stansberry has a similar theory on gold's rise but the method or reasoning behind is a little different. Stansberry mentions that the US dollar could collapse and banks could close. When banks close there will be panic and nobody will have access to their money. This is why the #1 method is to hold cash first. Once banks close and nobody can get their cash, Stansberry suggests the only way to restore confidence in the US dollar and banks is to back it by gold.

Not a 1:1 ratio, but pegged to the dollar, similar to when gold backed our currency in 1971. For this to work, given the amount of US dollars in circulation now, Stansberry says gold would need to rise to $10,000 an ounce.

I'm not suggesting the end of the world is coming; just a pop in the bubble of the US dollar and other paper currencies. When that happens, it will be the end of the financial world.

Gold is a currency. It has acted as a currency, never once failing through all of history. The reason most people (including Warren Buffet) bash gold is because it earns no return. There is no dividend. There is no interest. You just hold it, earn nothing, and wait for the price to rise.

This is all true. But it's the only currency that will survive the upcoming financial crisis in its current form. It serves as financial insurance. When there is complete panic in the stock market, bond market, and currency markets; money will rush to gold for safety.

This is what led to the spike we had in gold at the beginning of 2016. The fed raised interest rates in December 2015, China devalued their currency, and the stock market dipped. Money poured into gold.

When everyone thought the UK would vote to remain in the EU and "Brexit" won (leaving the EU), gold spiked overnight as money rushed into safety. When investors first realized Trump was going to win— late Tuesday -- gold spiked overnight as money rushed into safety. Ultimately in both scenarios, this reversed, but the point is that when there is a crisis and uncertainty, money rushes to the safety of gold.

I have no idea if Jim Rickards and Porter Stansberry will be right in how the price of gold will go up or how much it will go up. But I do know when there is a financial crisis, money will rush to gold driving it much, much higher.

And you don't need all that much for protection. As little as 10% of your portfolio can protect you from the collapse of the dollar and the coming financial crisis. Let's say the value of the dollar drops to 1/5th its value. And stocks, bonds, real estate all drop by 5. In other words, $100,000 drops 80% down to $20,000. Gold could go up by 500%. $100,000 could become $500,000.

Say you have a $200,000 portfolio with 10% in gold ($20,000). If the rest of your portfolio drops in value by 80%, from $180,000 down to $36,000 you've just lost $144,000. However if gold then goes up by 500% from $20,000 to $100,000 you just made $80,000. Your portfolio now only lost 32% instead of 80% just by having 10% allocated to gold.

Right now, gold is extremely cheap. Your long term asset allocation strategy should have 10-20% allocated to precious metals according to my *Let Your Asset Allocation Build* strategy. Gold is:

* Cheap
* The only currency that will survive the coming crisis in its current form
* Great financial insurance

For these reasons, I believe you should have at least 20% of your portfolio in gold.

Under the scenario above, you'd have $40,000 in gold and $160,000 in everything else. That $160,000 would drop down to $32,000. But gold would go from $40,000 to $200,000. Your portfolio would go up by 16% with just a 20% allocation to gold, while everything else dropped 80%!

So you can easily protect yourself with only a 20% allocation to gold.

Why Gold Is Extremely Cheap

Gold is a commodity and goes through the same booms and busts as other commodities. Gold should have been going up over the last several years as we increased the money supply though QE with a suffering economy, but it didn't. It didn't because mainstream media and financial outlets don't make money off you owning gold. So they bashed gold and wanted you in stocks since they were going up and that's how they make money.

Gold boomed coming out of the last financial crisis, making it all the way to $1,900 an ounce. But then when everyone became comfortable that we could get markets going higher, it dropped down to around $1,000 per ounce. Since it's a commodity you have to explore and mine for it, and with the price dropping into bust territory there was no money to explore. Mines closed and production dropped drastically.

This is a perfect example of how to make money on commodity cycles. When all the money comes out, nobody wants to buy and the sector is hated. This creates our opportunity. When nobody wants to buy, the price can only go up. And it's going to go up as demand increases as more and more people want safety during the upcoming crisis. Be a contrarian. Think differently than the 99%, mainstream media, and financial advisors.

Gold should have been going up because of the continued attempts to inflate paper money through QE and low interest rates but financial institutions and the media have dismissed it as unneeded, and so it actually has gone down, even as the supply chain has diminished. This sets up a dynamic bottleneck.

When the financial crisis hits and the US dollar collapses there will not be enough gold. And you cannot mine it overnight. You have to explore for it, get environmental approvals, build mines, and then actually mine it. This takes years. When the demand spikes supply will not be able to keep up. This will drive the price much, much higher.

So even if Jim Rickards and Porter Stansberry are wrong with their predictions, gold demand will soar and simply because of reduced supply, the price will skyrocket.

Gold prices have moved between $1,100 and $1,375 the last half of 2016. It's been moving up and down based on talks of raising interest rates. You should ignore all of this and just start buying gold to reach a minimum of 20% allocation over the next 6 months. When you see a big drop, buy a third of what you need. Then another third when it drops again. And the last third when it drops again. Don't worry about trying to time the bottom. Just know gold is going to protect your portfolio and going to go much, much higher.

A great quote regarding when to buy gold and not worrying about short term corrections from the *Stansberry Digest*, "The risk of not owning enough gold is far greater than the risk of buying before a short term correction."[26] Remember, we're in this for the next 3-7 years and for accelerating our long term wealth building.

Now if you're still in the wealth building stage like I am and nowhere near your long term portfolio goal, my *Let Your Asset Allocation Build* strategy will recommend you to go overweight in gold.

It's so cheap, has such little risk of going lower (it's at the bottom of a commodity cycle), and such high probabilities of going much, much higher over the next 5-10 years, I'm extremely overweight in gold (in the short term but not in my long term asset allocation).

I own some stocks but nowhere near the allocation I ultimately want because they are too expensive. I own zero bonds because they are way too expensive. I own some rental real estate but that is more part of a business I'm creating because true investment properties are getting expensive.

Gold is cheap so I'm loading up now. You can also buy some of gold's sister, silver. I own some silver and a lot of gold.

You can buy gold bullion or you can buy gold exchange traded funds (ETF's). Just be careful when buying gold ETF's to not pay over the net asset value (NAV). The net asset value is what the exchange traded fund would be worth if the fund liquidated its assets at the current spot price. Sometimes funds trade above this NAV so you're actually paying more than the spot price of gold. However, some funds trade below, so you're actually paying less than the spot price of gold.

I recommend having some physical gold and some gold ETF's. I have both. If you want specific recommendations on what ETF's or type of coins to buy, please see Appendix 3 for specific newsletters that can guide you.

---

26 Justin Brill. Stansberry Digest. May 26, 2016. "What to do if you missed the Gold Rally."

Find a gold dealer you can trust, ask your broker for some gold funds, or do a little research to find the gold funds on your own. Then buy some gold today. Don't wait until things get worse. Remember, to get ahead we need to take action contrary to what everyone else is doing before everyone else wants to do it.

Note: Gold is considered a collectible and in taxable accounts, gains are taxed at a maximum 28% when you sell. This includes physical bullion and gold ETF's. For more information, please read the tax report that can be purchased from my website, www.coast2coastfinancial.com. There are ways around this higher tax but you need to review what's in the guide and consult with your tax advisor.

#3 Method to PROTECT Yourself during the Coming Financial Crisis: Dump Bonds

Get out of any bonds that are not top investment grade or highly rated municipal bond funds. I'm not going to spend a lot of time on this because we already discussed why the bond market could collapse at any moment. We've also mentioned why low investment grade is actually becoming part of the high-yield "junk bond" segment. Call your finial advisor or check the holdings of funds in your retirement account. Make sure you are only holding bonds higher than BBB grade.

Even the price of these bonds could crash, but most likely the companies will not default. So if you are holding to maturity, which you should be in your retirement account, you can wait out the duration of the bond and not worry about the price dropping.

If you own municipal bonds, make sure you own a fund. Municipal bonds may also have defaults but if you own a portfolio across high graded municipalities, you should be fine. Remember municipals have the ability to tax to make payments and will pay bonds before they pay pensioners and other obligations. But if you own just one municipal bond and it defaults, you could be in trouble.

#4 Method to PROTECT Yourself during the Coming Financial Crisis: Quality Stocks

Only own quality dividend paying or value stocks you're confident will survive and pay dividends or go up over the long term (10-15 years). And don't sell in a panic when the stock market crashes. Have conviction in your stocks and hold them. Remember selling low is what most people do. If you bought these stocks at a good price, hold them, collect dividend payments and wait for prices to come back over the long-run.

I don't recommend buying many new stocks today unless you do your homework or subscribe to a newsletter that is recommending only value or cheap dividend-paying stocks to hold for the long term. I'm recommending you only own stocks you bought previously at a good price.

These are stocks you believe will last through any recession and always be around. Coke is the example I used earlier. I'm not going into a lot of detail because I can't discuss individual companies or recommendations. However in Appendix 3, there are some great newsletters that recommend good income paying stocks and value stocks you can buy and hold for the long term.

Get out of all other stocks. In your retirement accounts, if you cannot own individual stocks, make sure you own large cap dividend paying funds. Or large cap value funds. And don't sell at the bottom. You only sell these companies if the underlying fundamentals of the company deteriorate. You don't sell when everyone else is selling in a panic.

This is when you buy to make a fortune, which leads us to…

#5 Method to PROFIT during and After the Coming Financial Crisis: Gold Mining Stocks

Own gold mining stocks and junior gold explorer stocks. These stocks carry much more risk than owning physical gold or gold EFT's. But when gold runs higher, these stocks will go both higher and faster. But the risk is much greater as well. Don't own just one or two of these because they are more likely to go bankrupt. You need to own a basket or fund of these.

In the Appendix 3, I'll refer to several newsletters that provide specific recommendations on gold mining stocks to buy, and also provide how you should allocate amongst them.

Since gold is so cheap and we're in our wealth building stage, I'd allocate 10-20% to these stocks— more to the big mining stocks and royalty companies and less to the riskier junior stocks. But if you want to get ahead, owning these is a must.

Let me explain how they can be SO profitable. If a miner produces gold for $800 an ounce and it's trading at $1,000 per ounce, they make $200 of earnings. But a bump in gold price dramatically boosts both earnings and stock price.

If gold rises from $1,000 an ounce to $5,000 an ounce that is a 500% gain in gold. However the gold miner's profits just went from $200 an ounce to $4,200 an ounce ($5,000 minus $800). That's a 2,100% increase in profits! The stock price based on a multiple of earnings could also go up 2,000%. This is how you really profit off the coming crisis, the collapse in paper currencies, and the gold bull market.

I am personally invested in gold stocks recommended by all the newsletters I mention in the Appendix 3.

#6 Method to PROFIT during and After the Coming Financial Crisis: Keep Cash in Portfolio

Have cash in your portfolio. Again this may sound contradictory. But it's necessary to have cash to take advantage of the opportunities that will arise.

Personally my portfolio is mostly gold and gold miners, some value and dividend stocks, and cash. Bonds are too expensive right now but will become cheap. Most great quality dividend stocks like Coke are expensive right now, but will become cheap. Technology companies like Amazon are expensive right now but will become cheap.

When markets fall and selling begins, everything goes down. We'll protect ourselves with cash saved at home and our portfolio heavily weighted in gold. By selling off expensive stocks and bonds and raising cash, we'll be able to buy into the incredible deals that will become available.

Not only will gold mining stocks make us a ton of money over the next 3-7 years, we'll have cash to buy into great dividend paying stocks and value stocks which will make us a fortune for the 15-20 years after that.

If you don't have cash, you can't take advantage of this opportunity. Remember back in 2009, there was an opportunity to buy great companies on the cheap. But you had to be prepared to do so. You had to have the cash and the conviction to buy. After reading this book you should have the conviction. Now you need to make sure you have the cash.

Yes, this cash will become worth less as the dollar collapses, but it is still worth holding to take advantage of these deals. And remember your gold allocation will offset any losses in this cash, allowing you to buy great companies that pay amazing dividends on the cheap.

As these opportunities arise I'll inform you through my newsletter and through a new report or book. Most likely it will be exactly when everyone else you know, mainstream media, and financial advisors tell you not to buy stocks. Because everyone will have just lost a ton of money during the crash. But you won't. You'll have profited!

#7 Method to PROFIT during and After the Coming Financial Crisis: China

I'm only going to briefly touch on this opportunity. This idea is not the purpose of the book and is only for those who have more investable funds. This is not essential, but if you have more funds after following the previous items, I highly recommend this.

For more details you will have to read the Appendix 3 and subscribe to *True Wealth China Opportunities.*

As I mentioned earlier, China is the world's second largest economy and on a mission to become a world power. It just went from being excluded from the IMF's SDR basket to becoming the 3rd highest weighting out of 5.

It also went from its stock market being unrecognized worldwide to getting added to the MSCI emerging markets index.

On top of that, China is in the early stages of a technology boom like the US boom of the past 15 years. If you missed out on Facebook, Amazon, and all the big new technology stocks in the US, they are still cheap in China. And they have the potential to go even higher because China has substantially more people.

China is not going away regardless of your feelings about China. They are investing heavily in new technology, military equipment, and renewable energy. The media and financial outlets hate China because they're worried about their rise to power. They'll tell you all about "ghost cities" and how China is in a bubble. Don't let this emotion and American pride stop you from taking advantage of this opportunity.

#8 Method to PROFIT during and after the Coming Financial Crisis: The Big Short

The last method I'm going to touch on only lightly. For those of you who have more investing experience and more capital available, this is another speculative option for making huge gains.

You'll have to go to the Appendix 3 and subscribe to Stansberry's *Big Trade* to get the specifics.

This idea is to short (sell puts) overvalued and indebted companies that will crash during the coming bond market default cycle. Stansberry has reviewed companies with bonds that are highly likely to default. If they do, their stock price will crash and you could make huge gains. If this appeals to you, check out the newsletter for more information.

Conclusion: I hope this material was laid out plainly and simply and you learned a lot. I hope you enjoyed reading and are motivated to take action.

It's not difficult to immediately buy gold and save cash. If you are unsure how to do it, spend a little money and subscribe to *Stansberry's Gold and Silver Advisory*. They will give you simple steps to implement.

If you don't have much money saved or only have money in your 401(k) or other retirement accounts please be sure to read Appendix 1.

I do not promise anything in this book will happen exactly as described, that would be impossible. But I believe strongly that if you understand this book, take action and implement the strategies in your portfolio today, you'll greatly outperform everyone else over the next 3-7 years. And you'll create an opportunity to really get ahead and supercharge your retirement.

Remember, the way this is most likely going to first play out will appear to contradict what I've told you. Especially if you only listen to the 99%, mainstream media, and financial outlets, you'll get lulled to sleep. You'll see the stock market going higher, the US dollar strengthening, and gold beginning to decrease. It'll appear that I'm completely wrong on the surface.

But if you understand this book, follow my newsletter, and think outside of the mainstream you'll understand what's really happening. Greed is driving these things into an enormous bubble. And mainstream media and financial outlets are fueling this greed, even reinforcing it. This is when bubbles pop. Prepare yourself now and ignore all the false messages. Trust that in 3-7 years you'll see the crisis unfold. Then, you'll not only be protected and profit, you'll have cash to buy assets on the cheap to profit during the next boom! ... And the next boom WILL come.

You deserve credit for reading this book and working to understand it. I tried to leave out charts and stats as much as possible because I wanted to stick with the essential message. I read charts and details because I enjoy it. I just want you to easily understand what's going on so you can protect, profit, and spend your time doing what *you* enjoy. That's how we make the world a better place.

Please keep up to date by reading my weekly newsletter and special reports. I'll let you know what's really happening in a simple, easy-to-understand manner. I won't give you the same misleading information you hear on the news or your financial advisor tells you. I'll listen to that information and read all of my paid-for financial research. Then I'll process it, and cut to the chase for you so you can spend just 20 minutes a week reading and know ways to protect and build your wealth.

Congratulations for reading to the end of the book. I will reward you with the asset allocation I gave my close personal friends. I'm 35 and most of my friends are the same. We have a long time to *Let Your Asset Allocation Build*, but if you read that report, you'll understand the best way to reach your retirement goal if you're early in the wealth building process. Follow this **only** if you do agree with and are comfortable following my proprietary asset allocation strategy and are willing to commit up to 10 years of disciplined investing and holding. If not, **do not follow this allocation**.

Gold/Silver: 50% (25% pure bullion, 15% mining stocks, and 10% junior mining stocks) subscribe to *Stansberry Gold and Silver Advisory* for specifics.

Cash: 20%

Income: 15% (quality dividend stocks, municipal bond funds, Real Estate Investment Trusts, and high quality investment grade bond funds) subscribe to *Income Intelligence* for specifics.

China's stocks: 15% subscribe to *True Wealth China Opportunities* for specifics.

Dear Investor,

Please email me any feedback, questions, or advice for future reports and newsletters to feedback@coast2coastfinancial.com. I read all emails and will respond to common questions in my weekly newsletter.

To your wealth, health, and personal freedom.

Thanks for reading.

Chad A. Walker, CPA, MBA

Appendix 1: Ways to Use Your 401(k) or IRA If You Have No Savings

If you have little cash and investable assets saved outside of your retirement account, here are ways you can implement the gold strategy in your retirement accounts. There is a great advantage to this. When you use your IRA, 401(k) or better yet, ROTH IRA or 401(k), you can avoid the higher maximum 28% collectible tax on profits in gold.

The downfall is, your retirement account may limit your ability to implement this strategy. But with a little work you may be able to get around it.

First, if your employer contributes any sort of match to your 401(k), I suggest you contribute as much as you can get matched. If your employer is offering you free money, take it!

I've seen some employers contribute a 100% match up to your first 6%. If so, contribute 6%. I've seen employers contribute an 80% match up to 6%. If so contribute 6%. I've seen employers contribute a 50% match up to 6%. If so contribute 6%.

The point here is that if you're getting any sort of match from your employer, up to a specific percentage, contribute that percentage.

But after that, I move away from most mainstream financial advice. Don't contribute above the percentage your employer provides a match. Take full advantage of the free money but don't contribute any more. Most financial outlets tell you to contribute as much as allowed by law to take advantage of the tax breaks. I disagree.

Most employer 401(k) plans offer a limited amount of funds that you can choose for your investments. These are typically restricted to large cap stocks, small cap stocks, international stocks, bonds, and money markets funds.

I've seen the investment offerings in a lot of different 401(k)'s and most are limited to that small range of investments. This is good for the financial companies that run those mutual or index funds but bad for you. If you're limited to those investments, how can you implement the needed strategies to maximize your wealth building?

If stocks and bonds are all really expensive right now, you are forced to overpay for any investment you make. Or you're forced to just sit in a money market which is almost as bad.

You're better off just taking the free money (we'll talk about how to invest the free money below if you're restricted to just these options) and contributing to an IRA that allows you to buy the individual stocks or ETF's you choose. Better yet, get a self-directed IRA that allows you to buy rental real estate and gold bullion. If you choose to invest after taxes, use a ROTH IRA to maximize your returns. I think you're better off putting the minimum matched in a tax deferred 401(k) then paying tax on the remaining investment money now and investing it properly.

So what to do if you have money already in a 401(k) that has these limited investment options?

Option #1:

First, have you left your job where this money was contributed? If you did, you should be eligible to roll your 401(k) over into an IRA that allows you to invest in individual stocks and ETF's. This is very standard and I've done this myself several times.

Fidelity makes this very simple for you to do and also only charges $7.95 commission on each trade. I receive no compensation from Fidelity, I just personally use them for my retirement accounts and it's been easy. If you call them up, within 15-20 minutes they'll walk you through how to create an IRA and roll your old 401(k) into the IRA. Just make sure you know your account number of the old 401(k) or IRA the funds are sitting in.

If you haven't left your job or your new job has the majority of your money in its 401(k) with limited options there are other steps you can take.

Option #2:

If you work for a really large company, your employer's 401(k) may offer something referred to as BrokerageLink®. Depending upon the broker your employer uses it may have a different name. Again, I have Fidelity and work for a large employer and it's called BrokerageLink®.

What BrokerageLink® does is it allows you to move some percentage of your 401(k) funds out of the standard account which is limited to specific funds and into a brokerage account where you can buy individual stocks and ETF's. The funds are still in your 401(k), it just gives you more investment options. Most likely they will not allow you to move *all* of your funds but I was able to move 50% of my funds into this option.

If you can do this, you can invest just as if the funds were in a personal brokerage account. You can buy gold ETF's, sit in cash waiting to buy amazing dividend paying stock opportunities, and/or invest in China. If the value of this brokerage account goes up significantly it'll reduce your opportunity to move more money into it. The way my employer plan works, I can't move new money into this unless I have less than 50% of my total value in this brokerage account.

I moved 50% into this as soon as I could and invested in gold. My brokerage account quickly went up almost 30% and now I can't move any more money in, until I contribute enough to exceed this 30% gain. I'm not complaining because I'll take the 30% gain but I want you to understand how this works.

If you work for a smaller company, this may not be an option so we will continue to get more creative.

Option #3:

The next option for you is to call your 401(k) broker and ask if you can roll any of your 401(k) into an IRA while still employed. I was actually able to do this with some of the funds remaining in my regular 401(k) that couldn't be moved into the BrokerageLink®.

Not all plans allow this and the percentage you can move varies but it is worth the 15-20 minute phone call to ask. I just called my broker of the 401(k) plan, they checked, told me how much I can move, and walked me through how to do it in a matter of minutes.

After these two simple moves, I basically had 75% of my 401(k) in a brokerage or IRA where I could invest in individual stocks and ETF's. I was able to implement my exact strategy with no issues.

Unfortunately for me the other 25% of my 401(k) is stuck in very limited investment options. And if you don't work for a really large company, 100% of your 401(k) may be stuck in very limited investment options.

Option #4:

If this is your case, what should you do?

This is tough. I don't know your personal situation so I can't give specific financial advice. But if you have over 20 years until retirement, here are my suggestions.

Step 1: Look and see if you have any precious metal funds available. If so, move 50% of your 401(k) into the precious metal fund. Make sure this fund owns gold and silver at a minimum.

Step 2: See if any general commodity funds exist. The entire commodity market has been in a bust for several years now. This includes coal, oil, soybeans, corn, hogs, etc. Over the next 5-10 years this bust should reverse. Put 10-15% into the commodity fund. If no precious metal fund exists, increase this to 25%.

Step 3: Find the large cap mutual or index fund that pays dividends. You want this fund to own quality stocks of companies whose products will be around for a long time. Stocks like Coke. I know they are overvalued right now but if you have no other options, this is your best option. These are going to drop in value during a crash but at least you'll earn a dividend while you ride out the storm. **Don't sell when the value drops during the crisis.** Put 15% into this fund. If you have no commodity or precious metal fund options, increase this to 50%.

Step 4: Take a look at the bond funds available. Are there any municipal bond funds or bond funds that only invest in investment grade bonds above BBB rating? If so, this is your next option. The whole bond market is probably going to drop but funds that are spread across municipalities or only top investment grade corporate bonds should still pay their interest payments as you hold to maturity. **Don't sell when the value drops during the crisis.**

Put 10% into this fund. If you have no commodity or precious metal funds up this to 15-20%.

Step 5: Hold the rest in cash. If you have precious metals funds and no commodity funds, that leaves you 25% cash. If you have both precious metals and commodity funds, only put 10% in commodities and you have 15% cash. If your only option is dividend stocks and bonds, you have 30-35% cash. When the market drops and we're in full panic and fear selling, don't sell. Invest your cash into the large dividend stocks first. Then put a smaller amount into the high investment grade bond funds. This will bring your average cost of these currently overvalued investments down to a more reasonable entry price.

Please make sure you understand these suggestions are for individuals with more than 20 years until retirement. It's based upon my proprietary asset allocation strategy as explained in the report, *Let Your Asset Allocation Build*.

If you have less than 20 years until retirement, or are not comfortable with this asset allocation strategy, please don't use the allocations recommended above. You can still use the different ways to try to open your investment options, but you must first determine the allocation that works best for you.

Don't let this information overwhelm you. Your 401(k) broker should be more than willing to answer any of these questions for you and help you quickly over the phone.

They don't need to know why you want to do it and should not try and sway you from wanting to do it. If none of the first 3 options are available for you, try asking this question: ***Is there any option available for me to buy individual ETF's or stocks?*** If they say no, I'm sorry. Then it's time to work on assets outside your retirement accounts. See Appendix 2 for help with that.

Appendix 2: Begin Saving Now and You Can Still Protect Your Money and Prosper

You may be saying, I don't have any savings. I don't have any investable funds. I have limited 401(k)/IRA funds and no options to invest in this incredible opportunity with gold.

You may be scared, frustrated, or worried after reading this book because you don't think you can protect yourself or take advantage of the situation in front of us.

If this is you and you have any of these emotions creating anxiety in you....

STOP!

Don't be scared or worried. Let the anxiety go and bring calm into your life. You can't focus on whatever has happened in the past to make the situation you're in now. Stressing over your situation won't help either. All you can do is begin to make your situation better. That is the only thing you have control over.

YOU NEED TO MAKE A COMMITMENT TO WORK TO IMPROVE YOUR SITUATION.

You may not like what I'm going to tell you next. You may think you can't do it. You may say it won't make a difference. You may say you can't do it in time.

I say BS. If you have this attitude, stop reading now. You need to take immediate action so you can protect yourself and even prosper.

I can't know when the US dollar is going to collapse and gold will march substantially higher. It could happen in 2017, it could happen in 2019. It could happen in 2022. I don't know. I just believe it will happen within the next 3-7 years and lean towards the earlier side.

Gold could go from around $1,100 where it is at the writing of this book to $1,500 in the next year. If you "miss out" on that rise, don't stress. That's just the beginning. You need to improve your situation by becoming disciplined before you can consider buying gold.

Here's what you need to do, starting immediately. I highly recommend you and your spouse (if you're married) read the books *The Automatic Millionaire* and *Smart Couples Finish Rich* by David Bach. They will help you see that you need to save money as your priority, first and automatically, then live off of whatever you have left.

Say you bring home after taxes, $2,000 a month. Immediately take some of that money and save it. Let's say $500. Then you need to figure out how to live off of $1,500 with no credit cards. Period. Don't develop a budget and save what's left over. You'll never have anything left over.

Figure out the amount you want to save to reach your short term and long term goals and live off the rest.

Here's my simple 10 step plan:

Step 1: Divide your monthly income by 4, after your 401(k) contributions— see Appendix 1. You're assuming 4 weeks per month. This is how much you have to live off of per week. Period. You can't spend more than this. If you really want to protect yourself, you must make sacrifices.

Step 2: Take $100 off of your weekly number and physically take a $100 bill and stash it in your home every single week. Whatever is left is what you must live off. If you want to protect yourself, you must be disciplined to do this. Do this every week until your cash stash equals 2 months of total living expenses.

Step 3: Make hard choices. If you truly cannot do Step 2 because you have "committed" expenses such as a mortgage, rent, car payments, credit card bills, etc., you need to change your life immediately or I can't help you. Sell your car, end your lease, and get a cheap car that you can buy with any cash. Would you rather drive a fancy car with no savings and no ability to protect yourself during a financial crisis? Or drive a cheap car knowing you're saving money and building a financial future?

I make a good living, have a nice savings, and feel completely protected and ready to prosper through the financial crisis. And I drive a 2003 Honda Accord with over 200,000 miles. Why? Driving a fancy car isn't moving me towards my goals.

Move if you must. Sell your home, move out of your expensive apartment and downsize. You don't need to "own" your home. Renting a small affordable apartment is fine. When I was in debt, I lived in a tiny bedroom with 2 roommates so I only had to pay $650 a month in rent in California. Then I lived in a small 450 square foot shack by the beach for $1,350 a month so I could live on my own but still save money. Now that I'm out of debt and am financially stable, I live in a nice 1BR apartment that costs $2,650 a month.

I had to make tough choices and sacrifices to get out of debt and get ahead. But I still drive that old car.

Step 4: Stop spending money on unnecessary things. You need to eat. You don't need to eat out. You may think you need coffee but the free coffee in your office works just as good as an expensive Dunkin Donuts or Starbucks's coffee. So does cheap McDonald's or gas station coffee. You can argue it doesn't taste as good, but get over it. You need to stop spending money on unnecessary things. Cooking is hard. I'm terrible at it. But sometimes you need to do it to save money. For almost 2 years, I ate Weight Watchers microwave dinners (that I always bought on sale) and a slice of buttered wheat bread for dinner every night. I made oatmeal with a little peanut butter for breakfast. For lunch, I drank meal replacement shakes or got cheap subway subs. I made sacrifices so I could get ahead. You need to as well.

Stop worrying about what other people think of your clothes. I wore the same blazers and dress shirts to work every day for over 5 years. Heck, maybe even 8 years. I don't care if someone thinks my clothes are out of fashion. My financial situation is in much better shape than theirs. Get over yourself and worrying about what others think. Stop spending money.

Step 5: GET OUT OF DEBT. In the Appendix 3 there are some reviews and references to a program to help you get out of debt. *The Automatic Millionaire* and *Smart Couples Finish Rich* books have good advice, too. Now that you've committed to saving and cutting expenses, figure out how to throw as much money as possible at your debts.

And don't get into debt ever again. Don't lease or finance a car. Don't use credit cards for vacations or purchases you can't pay off at the end of the month. Don't even get a big mortgage on the home you live in. All of these things are consumption. You shouldn't use debt for consumption. The financial and real estate industry will call me crazy for saying this, but financing the home you live in, is making you poor, not wealthy.

Buy a home to live in when you have cash. Before that you cannot really afford it. They tell you that you can. But look at the financing. It takes you 30 years and chances are you spend as much on interest as you did on the original cost of the house to "afford" to live there. I have debt on my income generating rental real estate. I rent where I live because I don't have cash to buy the home I live in.

Step 6: Once you're out of debt, increase that weekly amount to a $100 bill and a $50 bill. Learn to live off whatever is left. Go back and re-look at steps 3 and 4 again. Figure out where else you can cut and live off what is left.

Step 7: When you have 2-3 months of total expenses saved in cash and you're out of debt, use your $150 a week to buy gold. There is an easy way to do this when you have just a little money. Look at EverBank. (I use them but I receive no compensation for recommending them.) You can deposit money, and for as little as $100 a month, start a purchase plan in gold or silver. This allows you to slowly buy in and begin to build a gold portfolio. Each month, keep $250 in cash and put $250 a month into your gold purchase plan. Put $100 into a silver purchase plan.

Step 8, Option A: Once you save $5,000 cash in your EverBank account, open a brokerage account through them. Buy into a gold fund with $2,500. Put the other $2,500 into a gold mining stock fund.

Step 8, Option B: Once you save $5,000 cash in your EverBank account, find a coin dealer and buy gold and silver bullion. If gold is still under $1,500-$2,000 an ounce, buy 4 ¼ ounces of bullion coins. With the rest, buy 1 ounce silver bullion coins. I recommend buying Canadian Maple Leafs because they are pure silver and have a lower dealer commission over American

Liberties because most people think American Liberties are "better." This is not logical thinking.

If you go with Option B, once you save your next $1,000-$2,500 open a brokerage account and buy into a gold mining stock fund.

At this point, you're financially protected. And you have set yourself up to get ahead financially. This shouldn't be hard, once you read this and commit to a plan. It may sound hard and you may have hard choices to make, but if you do, you will get through these 8 steps before you know it! And you'll feel completely protected.

In my simple scenario from above, where you bring home $2,000 a month and save $400 to $600 a month, your total monthly expenses should be less than $2,000 a month. Otherwise you're living beyond your means and setting yourself up for failure. And once you save on average $500 a month, your monthly expenses should be less than $1,500 or you're living beyond your means and will never get ahead.

In this simple scenario, you'll have $3,000 (2 months' worth of expenses) saved in 6 months! If you have no debt, you'll have $1,500 in gold/silver and $1,500 in cash in your EverBank account another 6 months after that! In 1 year, you'll have 2 months' worth of expenses stashed in cash in your home, $1,500 in gold/silver and $1,500 in cash in the bank.

One year later, 2 years in total, you'll now have $4,500 in gold/silver and $4,500 in cash in the bank. At the beginning of year 3, you'll be opening a brokerage account!

Think about that, I think the crisis will hit in 3-7 years, leaning on the shorter side. Even if it came in a year, you'll already have living expenses saved and some gold/silver. And if it comes after 3 years, you'll have gold, cash, and mining stocks ready to start profiting and getting ahead.

With your cash, you'll be ready to buy an amazing dividend-paying company like Coke when that becomes cheap.

Step 9: Figure out how to increase your income. You can work more if paid hourly. You can make yourself more valuable to get raises if paid salary. You can start a side business. In Appendix 3 there is a great program that gives you numerous options to increase your income. And when you do, save it all! Keep building that savings and investable funds. Change your mindset to where more income does not mean more spending. It means more savings and investable funds to build towards a better future.

After 3 years, **congratulate yourself for what you've done.** Thank yourself for making the commitment 3 years ago to improve your future. **Plan a vacation that you'll go on in 6 months that will cost half of what you save during those 6 months.**

REWARD YOURSELF. YOU DESERVE IT.

Commit to continuing the course for another 3 years so you'll be even more prepared.

Step 10: Start learning about the next best cheap asset to buy. Hopefully you've been reading my weekly newsletter, *CPA Gone Mad*, and new reports during this whole process. If so, you probably have an idea of what's cheap. It may still be China. It may be something else. But begin using this extra savings from your increased income to figure out the next cheap asset to buy to continue accelerating your wealth according to my proprietary asset allocation strategy.

Appendix 3: Newsletter Recommendations

Trusted, specific recommendations, education on investing, and proven wealth building strategies

The law prohibits me from giving investment recommendations, mostly due to my role working for a large publicly traded company. This is why my book focuses on revealing what is happening in the financial area so you can understand the steps you can take to protect yourself and ultimately prosper.

Even though I can't give investment recommendations, I can explain what asset classes are best for your money to protect and profit. This is why I recommend gold.

Throughout my weekly newsletter and subsequent updates to this book, other book, or special reports I'll continue keeping you updated on:

* The macro view of what's happening in our world economy
* How it could impact you personally
* What asset classes you should be moving your money to in order to maximize the *Let Your Asset Allocation Build* wealth building strategy

I will also refer you to financial publications that I subscribe to personally, in order to obtain specific recommendations for my own money.

These financial newsletters must be paid for, but some come with free daily e-letters. Remember Chapter 1 about understanding the financial motivation of who is giving you financial advice. These newsletters do not receive compensation for you trading. They do not receive advertising money from funds, brokers, and advisors.

They receive subscription fees from individuals to whom they provide advice. Their financial motivation is to provide valuable advice that helps you to perform well so you keep subscribing.

Almost every newsletter offers full refunds within 30 or 60 days. And you can cancel at any time if you do not "trust" the information. There are a few exceptions that give most of their advice up front and thus will not give a refund. But they are very clear about their no-refund policy.

Below I provide the newsletters that I believe to be the best, most trusting, and relevant to what was discussed in this book.

For more information go directly to the newsletter publisher's site or give them a call. Please let them know you were referred to them by lifetime subscriber Chad Walker's book and that you'd like the best offer available to try their service that Chad highly recommends.

Caution: These newsletters make their living selling newsletters. So they send massive amounts of marketing materials in an attempt to persuade you to subscribe to more newsletters.

And they are great marketers. But because they offer free refunds and easy cancellation policies, you can try them without risk. Getting information different from what you hear anywhere else is important and the key to your ability to break free. They even publish reader feedback that blasts them for things they say. I laugh when I read most of these because those poor readers are so close minded they're going to miss out on one of the greatest opportunities to profit in our lifetime.

Just be aware of the marketing.

Even their free daily e-letters, which give great summaries of current events, have subtle, yet effective, marketing weaved into it. Don't get frustrated by this or sucked into it. Know what newsletters you want to purchase for your specific needs to take advantage of the current opportunity. Just skim through the free e-letters taking out the important educational information and ignore the marketing.

You don't need to subscribe to all their "hot" newsletters. This will only create confusion. I subscribe to them all, read and digest the contradictions, and help you understand the best opportunity for your money today, to build your long term asset allocation.

Also some of the newsletters provide recommendations monthly. This doesn't mean you need to invest into every recommendation. They provide recommendations every month because subscribers want a new hot pick.

They love getting a well written exciting story that comes with a recommendation they can buy every month. This excitement and buying of a new stock every month is what keeps that person subscribing. This is my major complaint with some of the newsletters. I can promise you I don't buy every recommendation.

How to Use Financial Newsletters

Unless the newsletter is specifically related to my top investment idea for the cheapest asset class to build my long term allocation, I don't read the letter immediately (For gold, I read most newsletters as soon as they come out because this is where 50% of my money is).

Step 1: I acknowledge there's a new newsletter, determine the topic by reading the intro, and flip to the end to see the recommendation.

Step 2: Most newsletters include a portfolio review. I scan this to see if any previous recommendations have become "better buys" or any stocks I own have become "sells."

Step 3: If any stock I own becomes a sell, I understand why and most likely sell myself. If any previous recommendation becomes a better buy, I consider buying depending on the next steps.

Step 4: I print the newsletter to read either during lunch one day, during an afternoon break, or on the weekend. Between now and then, I begin thinking on my own about why they may be making a recommendation in this industry, sector, etc. And why they may be recommending this specific stock.

Step 5: I read the newsletter and understand their full idea.

Step 6: I think about the idea for a short time and see how it compares with my initial thoughts. If my initial thought was this could be a good opportunity and the newsletter connects with that idea, I write down their specific investment advice.

Step 7: I review my portfolio and see how this recommendation would fit in my portfolio. Does it make sense for my long term goals? Even if it's a great idea, does it align with my specific long term asset allocation strategy? For example, would I need to move money away from the weighting I have in gold to buy this?

Step 8: I watch what the stock price does for the next week or so. And any related news that comes out. I think about it some more. I never rush.

After going through all these steps, if the stock fits into my portfolio and everything leads me to want the stock, I buy— as long as it's still under the recommended buy up to price.

Remember, these letters make everything sound exciting. They need to. That's how they sell newsletters. And most ideas are great ideas. But you need to make sure it fits *your specific long term goals*. I've found the best way to do this is by exercising patience and going through these eight steps.

Do I miss out on some opportunities that do well? Absolutely. Have I always been disciplined enough to follow this approach? Absolutely NOT! I've been reading and learning from these newsletters for over 4 years. I've learned from my mistakes so you don't have to make the same ones.

Last before we get into the newsletters, as I said there a few newsletters I trust greatly, and that align specifically with my long term asset allocation strategy. For those newsletters, I don't necessarily follow these eight steps. Since I know the newsletter fits into my strategy perfectly and I've learned to be trusting of the editor, I read them almost immediately and buy the recommendation.

Right now, these are mostly gold newsletters. However, I'm still buying long term value stocks and following two specific newsletters for a small portion of my portfolio. Remember, I believe it's okay to buy these stocks if you're disciplined to hold through the long term. And the other area is related to the incredible opportunity in China.

Note: Most of these newsletters are independent of each other but roll into the same parent of Agora Financial. This does not make Agora Financial a better publication than others, it's just the parent. Each newsletter operates on its own. Bill Bonner is the founder of this financial publishing giant and is one of the best daily reads I've yet to find.

Stansberry Research

This is the first company I came across and became a lifetime subscriber. I believe it is by far the best education I've received—even better than my college degrees. I don't buy a lot of their recommendations but I read everything to continue learning. The founder, Porter Stansberry, consistently says his role is to provide his readers the same information he would want to know if our roles were reversed. I've found this to be extremely accurate.

With any subscription to one of these newsletters, you receive the *Stansberry Digest* daily e-letter for free. I read this *Digest* almost every single day.

* ***Stansberry's Investment Advisory***: This is the flagship newsletter with Porter Stansberry as the editor. I own very few of the specific recommendations in this newsletter but I look forward to reading everything that comes with the subscription. It has a low annual fee and provides amazing education and insight into what's going on in financial markets. I'd recommend this newsletter to anyone who wants to learn, and, even if you don't buy a single recommendation, this is worth reading.
* ***Retirement Millionaire***: This is another low annual fee entry level newsletter. Written by Dr. David Eifrig. He is a former medical doctor and investment banker. Dr. Eifrig gives a boots on the ground view of the US economy and a sensible approach to building a great retirement. I don't believe I own a single recommendation from this newsletter but read it every month. Not only does he give simple views of the markets, he also provides tips on health and how to save money. This is a great choice for anyone who needs to save money and wants to learn to live healthier. You'll also get good insight into the financial markets.

* ***Income Intelligence***: Another newsletter by Dr. Eifrig. This newsletter is focused on income stocks across all sectors (Dividend stocks, bonds, REITs, MLPs, preferred shares, etc.). If you're looking specifically for income stocks, this is the best newsletter for you. I read and understand the ideas but this is not part of my current plan towards long term wealth building. This will come more into my focus as I get closer to retirement.
* ***True Wealth***: Another low annual fee entry level newsletter. This is written by Steve Sjuggerud, PhD. He has a PhD in finance and provides wonderful macro insight into the economy. His approach is unconventional but always an opportunity to learn. His recommendations are mostly funds as he does not analyze individual stocks, rather overall trends. I read this one, but currently this doesn't fit my plan.

Next up are the specific newsletters I'm following. I buy some of the stocks they recommend. These cost more but the information is phenomenal.

* ***Stansberry Gold and Silver Advisory***: Edited by Porter Stansberry. I follow this newsletter exactly. If you buy one newsletter to understand how to invest in the gold opportunity for protection and profit, this is the one. Not only does this newsletter explain in detail the opportunity that exists, it even breaks out a recommended allocation for your allotted gold investment. It breaks down how much to own in physical gold, large miners and royalties, and small junior miners/explorers. It even gives recommendations on collectible gold coins. The price tag is higher and it offers no refunds (you can cancel at any time) because it gives you the entire portfolio up front.
* ***Extreme Value***: This is one of the two newsletters I follow for the allocation of stocks in my portfolio. Edited by Dan Ferris and this is a high-end expensive newsletter. If you are just starting off on your journey, this may be too expensive for you right now. Build some wealth through gold; then subscribe to this. As discussed, most great

dividend paying companies are overvalued and I'm holding cash to buy them when the market crashes. But I still want some exposure to stocks so I'm buying some value stocks. I buy most of what Mr. Ferris recommends because I trust his judgment. He doesn't provide a recommendation every month because there are not enough value stocks to warrant that. I respect that discipline.

* ***True Wealth China Opportunities***: Edited by Steve Sjuggerud, PhD. I follow this portfolio as I believe the opportunity in China is incredible. However, this is still only for a small portion of my portfolio and if you're just working to build your investable funds, you should hold off on this. It's a higher-end publication that offers no refunds (you can cancel at any time) as it gives the entire portfolio up front. This is a long term play.

* ***Stansberry's Big Trade***: Edited by Porter Stansberry. This has only recently launched and is a higher-end publication with no refunds (you can cancel at any time). The focus of this newsletter is to short companies with large amounts of debt that are likely to default. As discussed above, this is a speculative newsletter and only for those with a large amount of capital available already. You can profit greatly from this but it is too risky if you're starting with a small amount of capital. Gold and gold miners are much safer speculations.

There are many other newsletters published under the Stansberry Research umbrella but these are the newsletters that relate to the strategies and themes in this book. My website will begin to add full reviews of each publication once I negotiate discounted rates for my readers. I'll let you know as soon as this relationship is established through my weekly newsletter.

Bonner and Partners

This publication is relatively new. It's directly run by Bill Bonner and his son Will Bonner. I'm only going to touch on two newsletters, one of which is a must read and includes no stock recommendations.

Through Bonner and Partners you can get the free daily *Bill Bonner's Diary* written by Bill Bonner. I read this almost every day and believe it gives the best insight into how the world and government really works.

* ***The Bill Bonner Letter***: Written by Bill Bonner. This letter gives no recommendations and is a low annual fee entry level publication. I look forward to reading this every month for the amazing insight into how the world economy and government actually works. Highly recommended for anyone who wants to learn more from someone that is not tainted by mainstream media and financial outlet bias.
* ***Bonner Private Portfolio***: The 2nd of two value portfolios I follow directly. This is edited by Chris Mayer, who Bill Bonner hired to write this newsletter. And Bill Bonner invests in these recommendations with his family's money. Mr. Bonner waits 48 hours after all recommendations before his family's money is invested. As mentioned above, a portion of my portfolio is still going to value stocks. This does not recommend stocks every month, just like *Extreme Value*, which I respect. I buy everything recommended, planning to hold through dips and crises.

Palm Beach Research Group

The Palm Beach Research Group has a monthly newsletter called the *Palm Beach Letter*. I receive and read this newsletter but do not buy any of the recommendations. My view is this newsletter is more for people closer to retirement and does not fit into my proprietary asset allocation strategy for someone who is under 40. I still read it as it provides unconventional investment options outside of the stock market. I like learning about these because I think they explain income opportunities to help me grow my income, rather than as true investments.

And that's why I bring it up in this book. If you're looking to learn how to save more money, increase your income, and need to build more wealth to participate in the ideas presented in this book you should check out Palm Beach Research Group and specifically....

* ***Palm Beach Wealth Builders Club***: I subscribed to this Club when I was over $200k in debt. Within three years I had a net worth of $500k. This didn't provide any magic formula and it was ultimately what I did that changed my situation. But what it did do was change my whole mindset on how to think about money, wealth, and happiness. It caused a change in behavior in me that allowed me to cut spending, increase savings, and create additional income. If you're an action taker, want to build more wealth, and are willing to commit to implementing ideas in this club, I highly recommend it. It changed my life and could your life too. But it only works if you take action on the information presented. Don't be overwhelmed by the volume of ideas to create additional income. Read them and decide which 2 or 3 fit your interests the best and begin implementing immediately.

* ***Legacy Portfolio***: I don't buy into this portfolio but I follow it. This is a portfolio of stocks that pay dividends, like Coke, that you should buy and plan to hold forever. It also has a proprietary approach to re-investing your dividends that takes a little more work but makes complete sense. Because I think these stocks are overvalued, I don't buy them today. But I follow this because I plan to buy as soon as they become cheap during the next financial crisis. It's these stocks we're holding cash to buy.

Gold Stock Analyst

This is edited by John Doody, who is considered by most industry experts as one of the best gold analysts around. He writes two newsletters that I subscribe to: ***The GSA Top 10*** and ***Fav 5***. The newsletters are very dry and only focus on giving specifics about the 10 and 5 mining stocks he recommends for gold and silver, respectively. Since I'm so bullish on gold, I buy whatever he recommends. He rarely changes his 10 and 5 holdings and just provides updates on the specific miners. This does not give a comprehensive review of how you should allocate your funds in gold like *Stansberry Gold and Silver Advisory* but he does give great insight into mining stocks. If you want specific recommendations for just mining stocks, I recommend.

Casey Research

I've only subscribed to this publication within the last year. What led me to subscribe is the founder Doug Casey. I agree with his political views on libertarianism and appreciate his take on the world. I don't follow any newsletter completely but do read the materials with great interest. There are two newsletters where I do buy some of the recommendations:

* ***International Speculator***: This publication is currently focused on the opportunity in gold and silver. It's not a newsletter dedicated solely to precious metals, it's dedicated to speculating. However, with the opportunity available in gold and silver as laid out in this book, speculation in small mining stocks is one of the best speculation opportunities available right now. Since I have a large exposure to Gold and Silver stocks through *Stansberry Gold and Silver Advisory* and *Gold Stock Analyst,* I don't buy everything. But I do read and buy some of the top recommendations or speculative opportunities available with a small amount of my portfolio. This is my "gambling money."

* ***Crisis Investing***: This publication is focused on what Doug Casey is legendary for in the investing world: Being a contrarian and investing where nobody else would. As of late 2016, I only owned one stock from this portfolio but I love reading the newsletter to learn more about how to look at investing where nobody else would consider. My belief is that the gold market, with its low risk, is the best place for my money today. But I do read this to look for incredible opportunities when crisis occurs, to buy stocks I want to own for the long term.

Agora Financial

This is the namesake publisher of the overall parent of most publications noted above. However, that does not mean you should think this is the best newsletter. I have it this low down the list because they have yet to earn my trust in specific recommendations. But to be honest, I've only recently subscribed.

That being said, Agora Financial has several newsletters written by Jim Rickards who I believe has incredible insight into the inner workings of the Federal Reserve, IMF, and governments around the world. I look forward to reading all of his 4 newsletters published under the Agora umbrella.

* **Jim Rickards' *Gold Speculator***: Since this is focused on gold, I read it diligently. Rickards provides great insight into the gold markets. This publication is specifically focused on small junior miners and explorers that could spike big during the gold boom. You should never buy just one of these and need to buy a basket. I've bought several (not all) of these with a very small amount of money.
* **Jim Rickards' *Strategic Intelligence***: I don't buy any of the recommendations but I love reading each issue to understand Rickards' take on what's actually happening inside governments around the world. If you're interested in learning more about this than the high-level views I share after reading all the information, I highly recommend this newsletter.
* **Jim Rickards' *Currency Wars***: This publication focuses on buying call options based upon the various currency wars occurring as discussed in this book. This is a more advanced strategy and I don't follow any of the recommendations. I consider this to be too much of a speculative move. But I read the newsletter because I love the insight into the currency wars going on and how this plays into the overall thesis of this book.
* **Jim Rickards' *Intelligence Triggers***: This publication focuses on buying call or put options to profit off specific short term moves expected from what's going on around the world. Again, I consider this

too speculative for my portfolio right now and don't follow any of the recommendations. I read it for the insight into what's actually happening in the world that you can't get through mainstream media or financial outlets.

The Oxford Club

I'll briefly mention this newsletter as it is not for the target market of my book. I only casually read some of the newsletters and follow none of the recommendations. In my opinion this club is for individuals with their wealth already established who like to learn more about how to manage and grow that wealth independently. Since we are still in the wealth building stages and under 40, this is not for us. I still subscribe and read casually because I want to understand the themes to be best prepared as I age and get closer to my wealth goals.

Early to Rise

I'm ending with a publisher that is not really financial based at all. This is a personal development publisher that focuses on social, health, wealth, and personal enrichment. It publishes a great daily e-letter that gives insight into personal enrichment and personal development. It has many publications that can help you become healthier (*Turbulence Training*), and to take control of your life to achieve your goals, (*The Perfect Day Formula*).

The *Perfect Day Formula* has transformed my ability to get more accomplished, relieve my anxiety, control my ADD, and achieve goals I knew were possible but was making no progress towards. It's this formula that allowed me to get this book written and published. I knew I needed to help people prepare for this coming crisis but didn't know how. After going through the *Perfect Day Formula*, clarity arose and I launched this book and newsletter.

www.ingramcontent.com/pod-product-compliance
Lightning Source LLC
Chambersburg PA
CBHW070028210526
45170CB00012B/379